D 802. F8
Rou

The Haunting Past

Critical Authors & Issues

Josué Harari, Series Editor

*A complete list of books in the series
is available from the publisher.*

The Haunting Past

History, Memory, and Justice in
Contemporary France

HENRY ROUSSO

With a Preface by Philippe Petit
Translated by Ralph Schoolcraft
Foreword to the English-Language Edition by Ora Avni

PENN

University of Pennsylvania Press

Philadelphia

10 9 8 7 6 5 4 3 2 1

Published by
University of Pennsylvania Press
Philadelphia, Pennsylvania 19104-4011

Library of Congress Cataloging-in-Publication Data

Rousso, Henry, 1954–
 [Hantise du passé. English]
 The haunting past : history, memory, and justice in contemporary France /
Henry Rousso ; with a preface by Philippe Petit ; translated by Ralph Schoolcraft ;
foreword to the English-language edition by Ora Avni.
  p. cm.
 Includes bibliographical references and index.
 ISBN 0-8122-3645-9 (cloth : alk. paper)
 1. France—History—German occupation, 1940–1945.   2. National socialism—
France—Moral and ethical aspects.   3. Holocaust, Jewish, 1939–1945—France.
4. Trials (Crimes against humanity)—France.   5. War criminals—France.   I. Title.
D802.F8 R65   2001
940.53′18′0944—dc21   2001037539

Contents

Foreword to the English-Language Edition

ORA AVNI

It is hard for an American to grasp the urgency of historical debates in French culture and politics. The United States started out as a country of immigrants. From the onset, individuals who came here from different countries and cultures did not share the same past. Their sense of forming a new community, their national identity and allegiance, rested therefore not on narratives of origins (which would have divided them) but on a shared project: building the future. France, of course, is centuries older. From early on, its very social structure relied on a feudal system which empowered the caste that could boast a certain origin— all the way to the king who owed his legitimacy to his lineage. Personal and national identities thus relied on a strong identification with a cherished past that guaranteed the social order and constituted the bedrock of the law that cemented French society. The end of the monarchy did not alter this principle. The nineteenth-century seesaw between republics and monarchies (or empires) engendered different historical narratives in which monarchies emphasized the continuity with the prerevolutionary ethos, while republics insisted on discontinuity and on the founding value of the Revolution. But with either version of history, France rallied around its past, its heroes, and its martyrs, and commemorated them with exuberant dedication and enthusiasm. Ernest Renan, still the cornerstone of France's political thought about nationalism, wrote in 1882: "The nation, like the individual, is the culmination of a long past of endeavors, sacrifice, and devotion. Of all cults, that of the ancestors is the most legitimate, for the ancestors have made us what we are. A heroic past, great men, glory (by which I understand genuine glory), this is the social capital upon which one bases a national idea" (Renan 52).

In the same vein, Ernest Lavisse, the most influential historian of the Third Republic, who wrote the official history textbooks used throughout France for close to a century, staunchly declared: "I know that if I denied myself certain feelings and certain ideas, my love for my birth place, a long memory of my ancestors, the joy of discovering my own soul in their thoughts and actions, in their history and in their legends; if I did not feel that I am part of a whole whose origin is lost in a distant fog and whose future is unknown . . . truly, I would no longer know who I am or what I am doing in this world. My life would not be worth living" (Lavisse, qtd. in Nora, *La Nation*, vol. 1, in *Les lieux de mémoire* 322; trans. Avni).

If one's very being is mediated by the thoughts, actions, history, and legends of ancestors, there is little to distinguish the past from the present: Both national and individual identities would draw on the shared past of a national community. In this imbrication of time frames, history simultaneously mirrors and shapes the needs and priorities of the present. Events that happened over a millennium ago can therefore still be the subject of heated discussions.

Take, for example, the hotly debated origin of France. Who were the first French: the Gauls or the Franks? Is the founding moment of the nation the first-century rebellion against Rome of the Gallic chieftain Vercingétorix and his sacrificial surrender to a victorious Caesar, or is it the baptism of the fifth-century chief, Clovis, who forcefully united most of the local tribes under his rule and converted to Catholicism? Trite academic quarrel? Not in France. Let me reframe the terms of the debate: Are France's unity and identity grounded in heroic resistance to a foreign threat (Us against Them), in a nationalist sentiment, or in the convergence of the political and the Catholic authorities (the well-trodden debate of the separation of church and state championed by the Third Republic)? Or again, was the nation grounded in the election of a leader by his peers (Vercingétorix), or was it conceived from the outset as a monarchy (Clovis)? These questions clearly dovetail with current passionate controversies. This explains why in 1996, as France was preparing to celebrate the 1,500th anniversary of Clovis's baptism, the politics of commemoration pitched Catholics against Protestants, Right against Left, the legacy of the French Revolution against various counterrevolutionary tendencies, advocates of the separation of church and state against those who would like to extend the church's sphere of influence (and its funding). The significance of the event was not lost on the Vatican: The pope set out for an unprecedented, well-advertised, and hotly contested tour throughout the most conservative Catholic regions of France still vividly remembered for their counterrevolutionary, anti-Republican wars (Vendée and Brittany). In a country where past and present circle in a merry-go-round, commemorations celebrate the historical narrative that best reflects the needs and priorities of the moment. Not only do each narrative, history, and commemoration reaffirm France's national unity and its historical continuity. They also constitute discrete political programs that up the ante of historical debates.

When Henry Rousso published *The Vichy Syndrome* in 1987, it met with an instantaneous success that extended far beyond the predictable scholarly circles. And yet Rousso had not set out to unearth new and sensational information about the painful 1940–44 collaboration of France with Nazi Germany—the way Robert Paxton had, for example, with his 1972 publication of *Vichy France: Old Guard and New Order, 1940–1944*, or Marcel Ophuls with the exceptional 1971 television documentary *The Sorrow and the Pity* (*Le chagrin et la pitié*). In fact, *The Vichy Syndrome* was not at all about the Vichy years proper. Rather, it started with the Liberation of France in 1944 and examined the various representations and perceptions of the Occupation until the 1980s. In addition to scholarly history, Rousso therefore examined film, national honors (such as elections to the Académie Française, and various literary prizes), fiction, public debates, commemorations, "affairs," and other media events. His project grew from the premise that what "really" happened in the past is no less valid an object of historical research than the subsequent accounts of that moment, since the disparities from one historical account to the other reflect sociopolitical and cultural evolutions that unquestionably pertain to the historian's domain and that are, moreover, themselves historically determined.

Notwithstanding its topical timeliness and exemplary analyses, the influence of the book extended beyond the study of Vichy to the larger question as to what constitutes an appropriate object for historical research in France. It underscored that not only is the writing of history accountable to the past, as elementary common sense would rightly wish it to be, but it also reflects the preoccupations and realities of the present or, more precisely, the preoccupations and realities of an unending series of "presents." In this, Rousso echoes Ernst Cassirer's view that "historical knowledge is the answer to definite questions, an answer which must be given by the past; but the questions themselves are put and dictated by the present—by our present intellectual interests and our present moral and social needs" (Cassirer 178). Of course, as the "intellectual interests" and "moral and social needs" evolve, so will the "answer" provided by the past, so that eventually we may face a series of such answers. This is indeed where the comparison with Cassirer ends, since the philosopher did not take into account that the more delicate and burning a nation's moral and social needs are, the more pressure there may be on the historian to provide a certain "right" answer, and the more likely it is that anything deviating from the public's expectations may well be ignored or even rejected.

The historical accounts of the Vichy regime are a case in point. Given the touchiness of the subject, French historians, intellectuals, politicians, and media churned out one history after another, each of which reflected a different set of intellectual, moral, social, psychological, and political needs. *The Vichy Syndrome* was as much a study of the evolution of these anguished needs as it was a study of either memory or historiography. The well-chosen word *syndrome*, which expressed the near pathological nature of the uneasy memory of the Vichy years and its complex web of symptoms/manifestations, was immediately adopted, thus providing a much-needed name for a burgeoning field of study in which Rousso has been one of the leaders.

In *The Vichy Syndrome*, Rousso identified four master narratives regarding Vichy, each attuned to a different set of social, political, and moral needs. First, liberated France tried to even the score by singling out for judgment (and execution) individuals who collaborated with Nazi Germany. In the next phase, as the nation set out to reclaim its place on the international scene and to recover from the bloody conflicts that had pitched Vichy's armed forces against the various Resistance groups (and, later, from the very divisive Algerian war), new histories were written that "repressed" the civil war and the Collaboration and proclaimed instead that France had stood united against the enemy. Social unrest kept mounting, however. It culminated in 1968, when the postwar generation loudly expressed its general dissatisfaction and clamored for a reevaluation of France's postwar social and political tenets. The passionate debates provoked by Ophuls's documentary and Paxton's revelations were in keeping with this mood: France's reassessment of her present had brought her to reexamine her past. In Rousso's terms, during this third phase, "the mirror had broken." More accounts of the Collaboration followed. Soon France was abuzz with the discovery of her less than glorious past between 1940 and 1944, willing collaboration with Nazi Germany, enthusiastic support of Pétain, anti-Semitic measures, policy of persecution and roundups of Jews, and especially her support of their deportation to the "East." Since the mid-1970s, the country has been in the thrall of anguished soul-searching and breast-beating. In this fourth and last phase, memory and the "duty to remember" ("le devoir de mémoire") have become a national obsession.

In 1994, Rousso coauthored a book with Éric Conan, *Vichy: An Ever-Present Past*, in which he returned to his analysis of the Vichy legacy to deplore the obsessional nature of the duty to remember. Forgetting, wrote the authors, is not the opposite of remembering. The two are complementary and interdependent. The duty to remember cannot therefore exclude forgetting lest memory be confused with obsession or fixation. A more integrated and comprehensive memory would put the dark years of Vichy in a truer perspective. To shore up this perception, they pointed at signs that the current highly selective duty to remember was beginning to cloud or even distort the perception of and reactions to the present. They reserved their most energetic criticism for the widespread confusion between memory and history. In France, they wrote, a facile popularization of memory had displaced the quest for factual knowledge of the period. Righteous indignation encouraged by the media had set in motion a series of "revelations" or denunciations. Public opinion had followed suit with demands of amends, reparations, punishments, and historical revisions. A cloud of generalized suspicion of French authorities (and of historians, accused of complacency) had descended on the country. Conan and Rousso went to great length to dispel what they saw as hype. They disputed the repeated claims that historians had failed to account for the crimes of Vichy and that it was high time the truth be known and justice be done. One of their main targets was precisely the slippage from truth to justice. Only the former, they claimed, was of concern to historians. Justice, on the other hand, is a matter of ethics or law, not history. The confusion between the two had driven the public to demand that historians draw clear lines between the victims of history and the agents of its evils or, worse, that they attempt to redress the wrongs of the past. The authors blamed the same confusion between truth and justice for the procedural difficulties raised by the sensational trials of Barbie (1987), Touvier (1994), and Papon (1997–98).

To better understand this controversy, it is useful to remember France's long tradition of staging spectacular trials through which con-

flicting views of national interest are hotly and often furiously debated
and in which the legal parties come to assume the weight of rival political agendas. One can cite early political trials like Joan of Arc's, which
unfolded within a web of conflicts, some of which were political and
secular (the House of France against the House of Burgundy, or again,
France against England), while others reflected the shifting power of the
Catholic Church, which was battling inner divisions and various here-
sies, as well as the mounting rivalry of secular powers. We can also
mention the eighteenth-century Calas affair in which the Calvinist Jean
Calas was accused by the church of having assassinated his son in order
to prevent him from converting to Catholicism and which, with the help
of Voltaire's powerful pen, became a *cause célèbre* against religious in-
tolerance. More recently, the Dreyfus affair called into question the integrity of the military, the judicial system, and eventually the republican
ideal itself.

In the twentieth century, the rumble of conflicting versions of history
echoes in courtrooms. In 1942, Vichy attempted to blame the Third Republic for the 1939 war and the 1940 defeat by staging the trials of some
of its most prominent leaders in Riom. After the Liberation, it was the
Vichy leadership's turn to stand trial. The collaborators' defense seized
that opportunity to put forth the "sword and shield" revisionist history,
by which Pétain's collaboration would have been a smoke screen for de
Gaulle's resistance effort. At about the same time, the storm surrounding
the Brasillach trial redefined party lines by going beyond the rift between collaborators and resisters onto a public debate about the political
and civic accountability of writers and intellectuals. With each of these
trials, what was at stake was, as de Gaulle would say, a "certain idea of
France" — be it in its relationship to the church, the Crown, its minorities, military, national interests, social makeup and values, its place in
the new Europe, its elites, and so forth. Revisionist histories were but
one of the ways in which such an idea of France was conveyed, authen-
ticated, and propagated.

In the past thirty years, as France was painfully coming to terms with
the Vichy years and as history was indeed rewritten, big trials became, in
Rousso's terms, major "vectors of memory." Time and again, the courts
were asked to straighten out the record and write the "true" history of
Vichy—especially regarding its responsibility for the persecution and
deportation of Jews—in order to teach the French public a lesson in
civics. That demand was less pronounced with the first trial: Klaus Barbie, a high-ranking Gestapo officer in Lyon nicknamed "the butcher of

Lyon," was German.[1] Nazism and the Final Solution had already been condemned in the courts and in public opinion. Barbie's trial did not inflict new guilt on France itself. But the next case went to the heart of the Collaboration. Bousquet was Vichy's chief of police when the French police rounded up thousands of Jews and sent them to French concentration camps, from which they were dispatched in cattle cars to the "East" (the infamous 1942 Vel' d'hiv' episode was but one in a series of such roundups). Since initially Vichy's measures against Jews did not constitute a legal category punishable by law, Bousquet was sentenced in 1946 to five years only of "national indignity" for complicity with the enemy. His sentence was immediately commuted, however, for "acts of resistance." He was free to pursue a brilliant and rewarding career in the private sector. Only in 1991 was he charged for the role he had played during the Occupation, but he was assassinated by a deranged avenger before his case came to court.

In 1994, Paul Touvier, a former Vichy militia man, was the first Frenchman condemned for crimes against humanity. Although condemned to death in absentia twice (1946 and 1947) for intelligence with the enemy, Touvier was still on the run thanks to the protection of high-ranking clergy in the French Catholic Church, a presidential pardon in 1971 by Georges Pompidou, and President Mitterrand's lack of enthusiasm for a vigorous prosecution of Vichy officials. Paradoxically, although it was intended to let the past rest, the 1971 pardon was instrumental in stirring up public opinion and in promoting the idea that it behooved the courts to make up for the government's reluctance to acknowledge France's tainted past. By the time his case was finally brought to court, Touvier was no longer charged with intelligence with the enemy (which had fallen under the statute of limitations) but with the execution of seven Jews (crimes against humanity), and he was sentenced to life in prison. He died in 1996.

Although his anti-Semitism was clearly proven in court, Touvier,

1. The difficulties in Barbie's trial were of a different nature. Due to the twenty-year statute of limitations on war crimes, Barbie could be prosecuted only for crimes against humanity on which there was no time limit. Stirred up by the incendiary maneuvers of Vergès, Barbie's attorney, the Resistance strongly contested the distinction between war crimes and crimes against humanity and brought up Barbie's brutal repression of their underground activities as well as the torture and death of Jean Moulin, de Gaulle's envoy and leader of the Resistance. Eventually an interpretive clause in the law was changed to allow for some of the charges. In the meantime, the legal debate had pitched the Jewish and the Resistance memories against each other and had exposed deep divisions within the Resistance itself.

however, had been a relatively insignificant player, a mere cog in the Vichy system. By the time he appeared in court, he was also a scared and barely coherent seventy-nine-year-old man, a pathetic figure who could not carry the weight of expectations that had been mounting for half a century. His sentence was incommensurate with the passions that had brought him to trial: Neither he nor his sentence could atone for Vichy's anti-Semitic measures.

Henry Rousso covered the lengthy trial for the newspaper *Libération*. In *Vichy: An Ever-Present Past*, he expressed his doubts that justice could be served after such a long time, exposed the procedural irregularities brought about by partisan politics, and voiced his misgivings regarding the pedagogical and civic value of the trial. By then, however, a much more important trial was coming. In 1981 the newspaper *Le Canard enchaîné* had disclosed that Maurice Papon, a high-ranking public servant under four governments (the Third, Fourth, and Fifth Republics and Vichy), prefect of Paris police under de Gaulle, and finance minister under Giscard d'Estaing, bore compromising responsibilities for the deportation of Jews from Bordeaux, where he had served as secretary general of the prefecture of the occupied Gironde region and as such had enforced measures against Jews, including their imprisonment and deportation. Under the pressure of public opinion and survivors' organizations, Maurice Papon was indicted for crimes against humanity in 1983. Due to the ambivalence of the courts and the authorities, however, the case was not brought to trial until 1997. In June 1998, the eighty-eight-year-old Papon was sentenced to ten years in prison.

Papon was a far cry from the insignificant Touvier. Not only had he occupied an important position under Vichy but he had been entrusted with important functions by every French government since then. For many, his success illustrated the deep complicity of French authorities in a cover-up of Vichy's role in the Final Solution. Papon's conviction, it was hoped, would be the conviction of the Vichy regime and by extension of France. Ostensibly then, the court's objective was to pronounce whether Papon was guilty or innocent of the allegation of crimes against humanity. And yet the media and the public kept clamoring for "history's trial." Public opinion wanted to see the history of Vichy on the accused bench at least as much as it wanted to see a highly placed collaborator on trial. Vichy's "state anti-Semitism" would then finally have its day in court, and history would have to reckon with the sentence. These expectations could only be met, however, if the court's role was not as much to judge an individual as it was to uncover and disclose historical truths and to draw a civic lesson from the past.

Leading historians of the Vichy years testified at the trial. Rousso was summoned by the defense, but he declined. Instead, he sent an explanatory note that was read in court and accepted by the presiding magistrate in lieu of his testimony (see appendix). The three interviews with Philippe Petit that form *The Haunting Past* could be read as an extension of that letter.[2] In the first one, Rousso attempts to wrestle the practice of history from the clutches of memory by underscoring the specificity of the tools and methods of academic history and by contrasting their rigor with the laxness of memory and with the passions stirred up by a sensational and often badly informed press. Cautiously and elegantly, he straddles the thorny line between objective and relativist history, positivism and constructionism, facts and their interpretation. This section could in fact stand on its own as a probing reflection on the craft of the historian and the social and cultural grounding of history.

The second interview extends the speculative inquiry to the history of the present, a lively specialty in France, represented by the Institut d'Histoire du Temps Présent (IHTP), which Henry Rousso has directed since 1994. It argues against the view that would limit historical investigation to completed and, therefore, past events. Since any investigation is necessarily filtered by the preoccupations and the demands of the present, temporal distance from the event under examination is not a guarantee of scientific impartiality. History of the past can be as biased and subjective as history of the present. Proper research, rigor, caution, and some degree of humility would better advance the historical project.

In the third interview Rousso applies the finding of the preceding analyses to two public events in which he was called to participate: the Papon trial, which was still not completed at the time of the interview, and the Aubrac roundtable in which he had taken part under the sponsorship of the daily *Libération*.[3] Since he was criticized for appearing at

---

2. Philippe Petit has written for *L'Événement du Jeudi* and *Marianne*. He is also the creator and director of the series "Conversations pour demain," in which the French edition of *The Haunting Past* first appeared. He has recently published *La cause de Sartre* (Paris: PUF, 2000).

3. Lucie and Raymond Aubrac are well-known resisters who have both written about their underground days. In 1943, Raymond had been arrested by Barbie along with Jean Moulin. He escaped with the help of members of the Lyon Resistance led by Lucie. She recounted the story of the arrest and the escape in *Ils partiront dans l'ivresse*, which in-

the roundtable and not in the Papon trial, Rousso goes to great lengths to distinguish between the two events.

His refusal to testify at the Papon trial hinged on his perception of the respective functions of the judicial system and academic historical research in a democracy. He argues that although they both strive for truth, their objectives and methods are different enough to bar crossovers. He focused on three major differences between the two. First, the court's foremost obligation is to judge, to issue a pronouncement of guilty or innocent, while the historian should refrain from judging. Second, since history is not a precise science and since it is by definition always subject to revisions, it should not be used in court with the certainty of evidence. Third, accepting a historian's "expert opinion" as legal evidence would constitute a synecdochic slippage from what could or might have happened to what actually happened, and it would preclude the vagaries of individual cases. A historian's testimony cannot therefore properly substantiate a verdict which must bear on one specific individual who acted under specific circumstances. It would compromise both the nature of historical inquiry and the integrity of the court, all the more so given the moral authority of history in France.

Here lies the difference between the Papon and the Aubrac affairs. The roundtable was not a trial. Although they pointed out some inexplicable inconsistencies in the Aubracs' accounts and asked for clarifications, the historians never attempted to reach a verdict. On the contrary, from the onset they had made it clear that they never gave any credence to the allegation of treason: They had already ascertained that the document incriminating the Aubracs was a forgery and that the couple was above suspicion. The Aubracs were clearly surprised and offended when the historians nonetheless pressed them for details. But despite some tense moments, the roundtable remained a discussion bent on understanding historical events, not on assessing individual guilt.

Ostensibly then, Rousso discusses a singular event in France, one that probably could not have unfolded in another country in the same manner. That much is indisputable. One might therefore be tempted to look

---

spired Claude Berri's movie *Lucie Aubrac*. In 1997, Gérard Chauvy published *Aubrac, Lyon 1943*, in which he cast the suspicion that Raymond Aubrac may have been the mole who betrayed Jean Moulin to the Nazi authorities (the document on which Chauvy based his theory is a known forgery probably written by Vergès, Klaus Barbie's defense attorney). Outraged, the Aubracs suggested a roundtable with historians from the IHTP and former resisters to clear their name. It was held in May 1997 and published by *Libération* on July 9, 1997.

at it as a strictly French phenomenon with little bearing on either justice or history as they are practiced elsewhere. It would be a mistake. Points of comparison are legion with, for example, the O. J. Simpson or Rodney King cases. More important, however peculiar we may find France's reliance on history and law, the fact remains that it is a democracy. Like other democracies, it has public institutions, some of which are intended to uphold the law and others to promote knowledge. Rousso's reflection on the practice of history and law and on their respective places among other democratic institutions therefore extends far beyond the confines of France. *The Haunting Past* is not only about a singular trial in specific circumstances. It is also about the methods by which we attempt to reach and frame different perspectives on knowledge and truth, the ways an open society can or should manage information, and the moral and civic responsibilities of the intellectual elite in a democracy. Few inquiries can match the urgency of the questions raised by this profound and brilliantly argued book.

Preface

PHILIPPE PETIT

The traumas of the past linger on because the nightmare of World War II
has lost little of its haunting power: Vichy, the Resistance, the Holocaust . . . Murky affairs from these difficult years jostle each other on the
front pages of newspapers. Curios and relics still draw crowds. In the
halls of Bordeaux's courts, the victims compete for legal precedence.
Resistance veterans take umbrage. Historians jump into the fray. In the
spotlight, Papon fights back. The righteous leap to their feet, while those
with compromising secrets slip off into the shadows. Through it all, the
government vouches for the legitimacy of the proceedings. The public
at large ends up baffled by the entire spectacle.

France is traumatized by its past, still unable to finish digesting the
"strange defeat of 1940" and the wounds wrought by French collaboration. This haunting past has become a national obsession. The generations born after 1945 tally up who died gun-in-hand, who resisted,
betrayed, just got by, or openly collaborated. Those who did not experience the war feign astonishment when told that the Resistance was
no different from any other human enterprise in that its participants
included people who were "disinterested and adept, heroes and go-
getters." [1] With great shows of contrition, they discover that the corpse
of Vichy is still warm and that the aftereffects of the war are incur-
able. Reliving it through the eyes of Lydie Salvayre in her 1997 novel
Compagnie des spectres, younger generations see the world in gloomy
shades of gray but Paris in black and white.[2] They no longer believe in

1. Georges Canguilhem, *Vie et mort de Jean Cavaillès* (Paris: Éditions Allia, 1996), 43.
2. In Salvayre's novel (Paris: Éditions du Seuil), an elderly woman is hostage to hor-

the brightly colored mirages of postwar reconstruction and "Republican synthesis."

Be they nothing but generalities, these impressions nonetheless are typical of the mood today. The memory of the tragic years from 1940 to 1944 has become a troubling issue with uncertain boundaries and aims. The frenzy of commemorations and the imperious injunction of the duty to remember have taken the place of political reflection. The undeniable, incomparable singularity of the Holocaust is "instrumentalized" toward partisan ends. The endless discussions over what meaning to attribute to the extermination of Europe's Jews border on Scholasticism. The historians and thinkers who dare "to face and accept the irreparable," who dare to look unflinchingly at what happened, are hardly legion.

Author of *The Vichy Syndrome* and coauthor of *Vichy: An Ever-Present Past*, director of the Institut d'Histoire du Temps Présent (IHTP) since 1994, Henry Rousso is among those who do not shy away from such difficulties.[3] Born in 1954 into a Jewish family from Alexandria that was forced to flee during the Suez crisis in 1956, Rousso understands the weight of one's origins and is no stranger to the anguish of exile. His way of looking at history and the misfortunes of this century is not bound up in a blind attachment to objectivity. By the same token, he adopts the attitude neither of a Faustian historian nor an evangelist believing himself to possess the ultimate truth. Rousso is a lucid scholar, conscious of historiography's limits but fully aware of its achievements as well. His conception of the craft is closer to that of Marc Bloch and Yosef Hayim Yerushalmi than to that of François Furet or Stéphane Courtois, director of *The Black Book of Communism* project. One does not summon history the same way one calls witnesses to the stand. As Rousso observes, the historian's work consists rather in bringing "the past into the present, but only to give us a better understanding of the

---

rors experienced under the Vichy government. Even fifty years later, this past remains permanently present for her—thus the title, which could be translated as *In the Company of Ghosts*. Impossible to corroborate, her recollections take the form of a delirium that contaminates her daughter's perception of reality as well. This occurs all the more easily given that the daughter was not yet born at the time of the incidents. Vichy is seen as the incarnation of absolute evil, with the occupying German forces largely absent from the account. Trans.

3. Affiliated with the Centre National de la Recherche Scientifique (CNRS), the Institute for the History of the Present is a leading research and archival center for the study of contemporary European history. The phrase *histoire du temps présent* is difficult to render accurately in English, for it suggests "the history of present eras" as well as "the history of the present." "History of the present" is preferred for its concision. Trans.

distance that separates the two and an appreciation of the changes that have occurred in the interim." Our obsession with the past is equaled only by its falsification or its "judicialization." Too many historians are tempted to write a "history where rhetoric gets the upper hand on argumentation." Too many journalists are prone to deciding from the outset who are the victims and who are the executioners, who are the innocent and who are the guilty. Events unfold as if it were necessary to exorcize the crimes of the past at any cost. We draw on memory and the justice system in an effort to do away with these wartime tragedies once and for all. For Rousso, it marks an attempt "to impose upon our unconscious a duty to remember," in much the same way as we are currently trying to impose upon history a duty to seek justice. The final irony of it all, notes French philosopher Alan Badiou, is that Nazism becomes "a watered-down term of judgment, applied here to Nasser or Saddam Hussein, there to Milosevic—in short, applied to all things considered unbearable and inhuman." 4

A consequence of this extended use of the term is that what is incomparable and singular becomes a dubious polemic concerning memory. Instead of identifying Nazism as a unique criminal political movement, we use it as a more generalized reference to concoct a historical notion of evil that is symmetrical to the transcendental notion of good. In so doing, we do away with the singularity of the past and present. It allows us to avoid thinking about the specificity of the extermination of Europe's Jews and to blind ourselves to the realities of the present day. In the name of morality, memory, and justice, we dissolve the historical singularity of events into abstract and circulating categories that render us deaf to the resonances of the past and the present. In the face of confusion on so many counts, it is important to get our clocks in order and make sense of these muddied questions.

Henry Rousso strikes us as ideally situated to shed light on these issues. It is time to learn "to live *with* the memory of tragedy rather than trying to live *without* it (as in the years right after the war) or *against* it (as we do today)." Work of remembrance accomplished without any thought of the future is wasted effort. Total forgetfulness and constant remembrance are two sides of the same deadly coin that prevent us from living and thinking. Having understood this before other historians of his generation, Rousso has set himself a code of conduct from which he

---

4. Badiou, "Lieu et déclaration," in *Paroles à la bouche du présent. Le négationnisme: histoire ou politique?*, ed. Natacha Michel, 177–84 (Marseille: Al Dante, 1997) 183.

has never strayed. In order to accept the irreparable, he has become a historian of the present. We have asked him to talk to us about the relevance of our past and to trace the history of this new discipline which took on a formal existence in 1979 with the creation of the IHTP. Papon, the Resistance, Vichy, the Holocaust—nothing has been skipped over. But alongside these controversial themes, we hope to provide arguments and answers concerning the proper use of memory, and perhaps by the end of the book the reader will feel a bit less haunted by the past.

Chapter 1
The Confusion Between Memory and History

Philippe Petit: When you were a student at the École Normale Supérieure in the mid-1970s, the discovery of Robert Paxton's *Vichy France* compelled you to pursue your studies on the history of the crisis years of 1940–44. With the publication of *The Vichy Syndrome* in 1987, you became a leading analyst of this period, demonstrating convincingly the extent to which France is traumatized by its past. Your refusal to testify at the Papon trial set you apart from your fellow historians. You are quite willingly an expert in this field, but you do not wish to become an "agitator of collective memory."

Henry Rousso: The recent past is presented to us today with unequaled intensity. It is receiving unprecedented attention because of our difficulties in facing up to the tragedies of the twentieth century. Only now are we coming to realize the true proportions of these tragedies. We are living in the "age of memory," that is, in a sensitive, affective, even painful relationship with the past. Like any citizen, the historian belongs to his age. But the historian must be able to consider it from a certain remove, establish a degree of detachment.

This is an essential part of any historical method: to help with this distancing. For a discipline such as contemporary history, as old as history itself but enjoying a revival of interest in Europe over the last twenty years, this effort is at the heart of its concerns. This approach, which we prefer to define as the "history of the present," turns the present—that is to say, the period contemporary to the actual participants and witnesses themselves—into a historical object like any other. From the very start, however, it has run up against events that seem to escape all rational explanation, with Nazism and the Holocaust foremost among them. The emergence of this field results from the pressing need to tackle this past, despite the tremendous difficulties such a task poses, with the will to analyze it rather than merely endure its effects. It is for this reason that the history of the present now has such a marked predilection for the subject of memory, undaunted by the methodological problems that face the attempt to do the history of the way societies live and think their own history.

The task is all the more ambitious given that the recent past is one of today's most hotly debated topics. It is not merely the subject of scholarly research and reflection. The recent past has been summoned before the judge's bench, as in the instance of the Maurice Papon trial, or it has been caught up in polemics laden with ideological stakes and issues of identity, like those related to the history of World War II and communism. In the face of such tumultuous echoes of previous ruptures, I believe that historians should refrain as much as possible from playing the role of "agitators of memory," if only as a reminder that history and memory should not be confused.

P.P.: The distinction established between memory and memories is a philosophical habitus. Memories designates the recovery of bits of knowledge or sensation, while memory signifies both the act of remembering and the past itself. When people talk about "historical memory," they often tend to confuse these registers. It seems that people would prefer that ceremonies of reminiscences be ceremonies of memory and that the past in general be forever present. You have spoken yourself of "la mémoire dans tous ses états"—memory in a state of commotion. As a historian, how do you explain this phenomenon?

H.R.: Today, regardless of the form adopted, acts of apprehending the past give rise to numerous misunderstandings, such as those you just mentioned. They result in part from a new, exacerbated sensitivity toward everything related to memory, one of the hot topics in contemporary public debate, in France as in other countries. The term *memory* is both omnipresent and polyvalent. It has invaded cultural and aesthetic vocabularies and is now a media buzzword. As soon as discussion turns to questions concerning the recent or distant past or to history in the most traditional sense of the term, *memory* almost inevitably springs to the fore, as if endowed with magical virtues and an aura of human spirit absent from history's accounts. And this is true of the most trivial as well as the most lyrical of circumstances. *Memory* is even used sometimes in scientific language in the most nonsensical ways, as shown in the recent debates about the "memory of water." The government also gets into the act: When the Social Security office tries to convince citizens of the usefulness of recording one's health in its new booklets, it presents them as the "memory of your health." Such metaphorical uses succeed perhaps in describing scientific realities for the public at large or borrow from the vocabularies of genetics and computer science. But they also grow out of a more general frame of mind particular to our era, a mind-set in which memory has gradually become a "value" and not just an objective phenomenon. Perhaps above all else, however, memory's rise to prominence is also due to certain reminiscences that still weigh heavily upon us in the ongoing aftermath of World War II and other twentieth-century tragedies. In Germany, France, and other nations, even the justice system has turned into a tribunal "to defend and honor memory," as with the belated trials of former Nazis and collaborators.

P.P.: Doesn't memory also figure prominently in political agendas?

H.R.: Since the early 1980s, both the French government and local powers have emphasized their claims to be carrying out a true "politics of memory" (which is itself the beneficiary of a new cultural politics). This is evident in the frenzy of commemorations seen for more than twenty years now. The development and promotion of museums, libraries, and now archives are other signs of this trend. In short, everything related to "patrimony," a concept indissociable from memory, has gained a new importance. The vogue of preservation in all its forms has spread to ever broader domains and objects—buildings, factories, or entire neighborhoods—as if the inclusion of the latter were a natural extension of the conservationist project. The desire to erase any trace of the past whatsoever is regarded today as suspect, regardless of whether the object to be conserved is beautiful or ugly, important or insignificant. Everything is susceptible to being "archived" and thus is potentially a "site of memory" to be established. The relative novelty here lies in the resolute, obsessive aspect of this attitude and in its pervasive dimensions, which now incorporate objects from our immediate daily environment in addition to traditional objects of conservation.

P.P.: Why such an obsession with the past?

H.R.: It is as if we lacked confidence and were unwilling to allow the selection of what must remain or disappear to occur spontaneously. This phenomenon is particularly striking in the case of the increasingly loaded notion of the "duty to remember." By this, I am referring to the way in which the need to know about or renew our memory of the tragedies from World War II—the Holocaust in particular—has been transformed into a permanent and urgent injunction, anchored in a new system of moral references.

P.P.: The term memory is often poorly defined, its use far from being clear.

H.R.: The current use of the term *memory* poses many problems. When we hear the word *memory*, it is increasingly difficult to tell whether the speaker means individual or collective memory, memory or history. In fact, *memory* is currently the predominant term for designating the past, not in an objective, rational manner, but with the implicit idea that one must preserve this past and keep it alive by attributing to it a role—without ever specifying which role it should be given.

Can one give a simple definition of memory? Saint Augustine explains the manner by which individual consciousness apprehends the measure of passing time: "Everything which happens leaves an impression on [my mind], and this impression remains after the thing itself has ceased to be. It is the impression that I measure, since it is still present, not the thing itself, which makes the impression as it passes and then moves into the past. When I measure time it is this impression that I measure."[1] Memory is therefore a phenomenon that operates in the present tense. The traditional image is of an imprint, an impression. Memory is as different from the past "as it really was" as the footprint is from the shoe that left it. But this is an active, living imprint, borne by subjects, beings endowed with reason and speech, and determined by their own experiences. Memory is a mental representation of the past, but it has only a partial rapport with that past. It can be defined as the *presence* or the *present of the past*, a reconstructed or reconstituted presence that organizes itself in the psyche of individuals around a complex maze of images, words, and sensations. It gives voice to a whole series of terms —memory, forgetting, denial, or repression—which do not mean the same things or obey the same mechanisms, yet imply an eventual return.

This brief discussion of individual memory is necessary because the current use of the word *memory* arises spontaneously as the contrary to "forgetting," even though by definition the latter should be considered (along with repression) as constitutive of memory. The contrast between the positive value attributed today to remembering and the negative value assigned to forgetting is thus in itself meaningless. It remains, however, an important element of the contemporary imaginary, and one must therefore take it into account in one's analyses.

---

1. Saint Augustine 276. Paul Ricœur offers insightful commentary in volume 1, chapter 1 of *Time and Narrative*. See also his recently published major work, *La mémoire, l'histoire, l'oubli*.

P.P.: "Forgetting" is most often tied to "forgetting misdeeds," to guilty conscience. In *The Vichy Syndrome*, you draw especially on psychoanalysis to address this aspect of the problematic.

H.R.: In order to describe the conflictual relations France has with its past, I have found it useful to borrow certain terms from psychoanalysis. It is less a question of offering a theoretical apparatus than of organizing a historical narrative with the help of a number of metaphors. In *The Vichy Syndrome*, for example, when I identify a period of "incomplete mourning" in the wake of the war, a period of "repression" between the 1950s and the 1970s in order to evoke the silences and taboos weighing on certain aspects of the Occupation years, followed by a progressive lifting of this repression which evolves into an "obsession" with those dark years—a phase in which we are still caught today—I transpose onto a collective level concepts which in principle can only be applied on an individual scale. But does this really distort our understanding of the phenomena? I am struck by how effective the analogies have proved themselves to be. They shed light on the connection between collective and individual trauma born of deportation and the war, trauma that could be analyzed clinically.[2] For example, many survivors of the Holocaust and other World War II tragedies were not able to carry out properly the process of mourning. In the years immediately following the war, they often were not ready to speak of these events, and the general public was not yet ready to listen. Over the last twenty years, however, their stories have found space for expression, an indication that a radical change has taken place in the social perception of the war years, as if perhaps the different "repressions" had finally given way. These psychoanalytic metaphors thus have their usefulness, though one must be careful not to take them too literally—borrowing terms of this nature, of course, has its limits. No one, for instance, has ever managed to provide scientific evidence of a "collective unconscious." On the other hand, however, to speak of memory is necessarily to bring into play the unconscious, which belongs not just to the register of the individual but also to that of social and collective phenomena. The words and images of our past and present permeate us as individuals just as they do the group or groups to which we belong.

P.P.: While we are on this subject, what distinction do you make between individual memory and collective memory?

2. A recent thesis in psychiatry by Jean-Marc Berthomé provides an interesting approach to both individual and "historical" trauma.

H.R.: Collective memory cannot be understood without reference to individual memory. Collective memory designates the living presence of the past on the scale of a given group, be it social (in the sense that one can speak of the "memory" of the working class), religious (the "memory" of the Jews, for instance), or national. Individual and collective memory share the trait of preserving identities. Both allow one to situate oneself in a larger temporal scheme, one that has meaning for the individuals—a tradition or a lineage, that is to say, a system of values and perennial experiences to which the passage of time has given a certain depth and breadth. By ensuring a form of continuity, both allow one to face change and the experience of otherness imposed by the passage of time. There is a proverb that states, "One cannot be and have been." Ever since Hegel, however, we know on the contrary that "to be" is precisely "to have been." "To be" is the capacity to imagine one's "becoming," to project oneself into the future. Neither individuals nor groups can live without a certain consciousness or approach to the past which allows them to situate themselves in time and space.

In addition, an individual experience—and thus a singular recollection—may eventually be passed on to others, thereby creating a social and collective bond. As a result, people sometimes fall into the trap of calling for the preservation of memories of events that they did not directly experience themselves. This means that individual and collective memory are in fact closely connected. Maurice Halbwachs was one of the first to draw attention to this phenomenon, just as he was one of the first to study collective memory, most notably in *On Collective Memory* in 1925 and *The Collective Memory*, published posthumously in 1950 after his disappearance in Nazi death camps. Moreover, it is striking to note that Halbwachs had few disciples until very recently. It is only lately that reflections on collective memory have made their way back into the social sciences and historiography. During my studies in the mid-1970s, for instance, I do not remember ever hearing the notion mentioned as a historical concept to be taken seriously.

Of particular relevance to us is Halbwachs's observation that individual memory is always inscribed in collective frames: one's family, school, job, or country. People do not remember all by themselves; they always remember *within a context*. One remembers experiences that end up having, in one way or another, a shared social dimension.

P.P.: And what do you make of the notion of "historical memory"? Though Halbwachs evoked it on occasion, he believed that the expression was misleading because "it connects two terms opposed in more than one aspect."

H.R.: Yes, it is true that Halbwachs made a distinction between historical memory and collective memory. The difference is in fact the same one that distinguishes memory and history, although the expression *historical memory* stresses that there is nonetheless a relation between the two, a hierarchy even. The distinction between the two terms is a traditional one even if today in common usage it has become blurred.

By definition, memory is based on experiences lived or passed on by others; in either case, it is a past that has left perceptible traces carried on within the living. History, understood here as a scholarly reconstruction of the past, focuses on individuals and social facts which perhaps have completely disappeared from collective memory but for which there nonetheless remain traces that the historian must spot and interpret.

The "history of historians" is an epistemological approach. It results from a desire for knowledge and obeys certain postulates and protocols. It is grounded in procedures for establishing verifiable and thus eventually refutable evidence. In its project of reconstructing meaningful temporal periods, history divides up the past according to rational or ideological criteria which can be very different from those of the contemporary agents themselves. Similarly, events deemed "memorable" or "historic" in their time can be seen very differently by historians. Moreover, both scholarly and popularized histories are narratives in the sense that they are passed on in the form of an organized story, be it closer to fiction or to scientific demonstration. This narrative thus possesses its own internal logic and discourse, both of which allow only for a partial vision of historical reality.

P.P.: This dilemma led Paul Veyne to say that a true history is unattainable. Couldn't one say the same thing about memory?

H.R.: Memory inscribes itself in the domain of identity and is a bearer of affect. It tends to reconstruct an idealized or demonized past. It can compress or expand time and disregard all forms of chronology (at least those which are rational). It is not an epistemological approach. Rather, it is part of our existential experience, those experiences which unfold largely outside of our control. Is it possible to control one's own memories or oversights? Can one control one's own unconscious—for instance, to impose upon it a duty to remember? One of the characteristics of memory is that it maintains continuity and enables individuals or groups to incorporate ruptures within that continuity. Halbwachs has called memory a "record of resemblances." Memory is on the side of the "same," whereas history is on the side of "change." Halbwachs's thinking thus moves along the same lines as that of Marc Bloch, who defines history as the "science of change." [3] In drawing on our imaginary, memory tends to bring us closer to the past, since it retrieves a selective, reconstructed portion of this past which informs our consciousness and present acts. Memory can also be seen as a burden, as when we speak of "the weight of the past." It is difficult to shed this kind of burden simply by making choices between what one wishes to remember and what one wishes to forget.[4] History, on the other hand, is supposed to bring the past into the present, but only to give us a better understanding of the distance that separates the two and an appreciation of the changes that have occurred in the interim. One could even argue that the only true lesson offered by history, or the study of history, is to achieve an awareness that humankind and societies can change (slowly or rapidly), and that even change itself can obey different modalities depending on the period. History is thus an apprenticeship in liberty, since the historical being is one who frees him- or herself from notions of destiny, be they divine or materialist, in order to impose his or her own path.

P.P.: But do you grant the possibility of a dialectical relation between memory and history?

H.R.: History and memory are not heterogeneous phenomena foreign to one another. Even though it is essential to distinguish between the two, the intellectual exercise of enumerating their differences or insisting upon their interpretative conflicts rapidly runs up against its limits. One can no more make a clean cut between history and memory than between individual and collective memory. This is even more evident in the case of the history of the present. The present is by definition a period where the memory of the recent past is passed on through the words of living individuals who directly experienced the periods on which the historian is working.

If memory is the affective, perceptible trace of the past and thus a truth of the present (or, *in* the present), and if scholarly history claims to restore the truth about the past, it remains no less the case that memory and history are also by definition "anachronistic." Both are situated

3. Halbwachs, *The Collective Memory*, 86–87. For Bloch, see his 1937 lecture, "Que demander à l'histoire?"

4. On this distinction, see Marie-Claire Lavabre, "Du poids et du choix du passé: lecture critique du 'syndrome de Vichy' " or *Le fil rouge: sociologie de la mémoire communiste*.

outside of the time frame of which they are supposed to render an account. It is more or less a truism to state that individual or collective memories and scholarly representations alike find their expression in a context other than the past. The narratives they propose are addressed to their contemporaries, in a language and a system of representations which are those of the present and not those of the past—even if one can find more or less striking continuities between the two. Like history, memory is a way to build a bridge between the past and the present (and thus the future as well). Quite independent of our capacity to remember, our interest in history signifies that there does indeed exist a desire to conserve ties to our distant past, including even that which has completely disappeared from collective memory. The practice of history is itself an anamnesis, a recommitting to memory.

Of course, scholarly history, and in particular the composition of national histories, is not without social and identity functions. Even if scholarly history has won the status of a social science in the course of this century and no longer accepts being confined to the edification of good citizens, it is also a vehicle for ideological (and thus affective) concerns. As a result, collective and historical memory overlap. To begin with, scholarly history is a vector of memory, that is to say, a process whose objective is to understand the past and to give it a certain intelligibility, along the same lines as other vectors of memory (commemorations, literary or artistic creations, and associations for veterans, ex-Resistance members, and deportees). This does not mean that one should confuse scholarly history with these other forms of remembrance, nor that their respective modalities and uses should be considered interchangeable. Like any approach that produces *knowledge* about the past, scholarly history contributes a specific and essential dimension. It underscores—and on occasion uncovers—individuals, facts, practices, and deep-rooted tendencies that contemporaries perhaps neither perceived nor understood. It casts light on features that only posterity and a retrospective examination can grasp. To confuse history and memory is to fail to recognize the fact that we remember and forget only what we have known and lived, not what we never knew.

P.P.: What does it mean then to work on the history of memory?

H.R.: Not all societies remember in the same manner, and not all of them have the same relation to the past. Over time, memory and scholarly history evolve, both in their context (their representations and interpretations) and in their means of expression (their ways of remembering and writing history). Thus, collective memory and scholarly history are themselves at least partially the result of a *history*, as paradoxical as that might seem. The same event or period will not have the same meaning a decade, century, or millennium later, an idea which is already generally accepted within the discipline. In one way or another, all historians are interested in historiography, which can be defined as the history of scholarly history. This allows one to study the evolution of historiography's own practices and the successive claims it has made concerning a given period or globally speaking. The same approach could be applied to the sum of social representations of the past and thus to collective memory, something which ethnologists and anthropologists have been doing for some time now.

Inscribed in the tradition of Halbwachs's analyses, this tendency coincides with the emergence of the very notion of memory in social and cultural fields. It sees itself as an opportunity to understand how collective memory functions today and in the past. It is also an effective means of doing the history of the present, since memory is a contemporary preoccupation. It is not at all surprising that the renewal of the history of the present and the emergence of a history of memory have been closely linked. Both are symptomatic of the "age of memory" that we mentioned above (even if neither are recent epistemological inventions). They demonstrate a desire to mark a distance not just with respect to the past itself—all historical approaches provide this—but with respect to the modalities by which contemporary societies understand the distant and recent pasts as well.

In *Realms of Memory*, for instance, Pierre Nora and his contributors provided a new and unprecedented look at the nature of commemoration in France over several centuries. The editors realized from the outset of the project in the early 1980s that we had entered into the "age of commemoration," as Nora's concluding article in the last volume of the series remarked. In undertaking the history of this process, these scholars not only developed a new scientific approach. They also cast a critical eye upon the present and the increasingly overwhelming weight of the notion of memory in our society. However, if we take Pierre Nora at his word, the results of this monumental study—or, rather, the *social effects* of this enterprise—were not at all what they expected. The notion of *lieu de mémoire* ["site or locus of memory"] was itself recuperated by the frenzy of commemoration. "The destiny of these *Realms of Memory* has been a strange one," writes Nora. "The work was intended, by virtue of its conception, method, and even title, to be a counter-commemorative type of history, but commemoration has overtaken it." Further on, Nora adds, "What was forged as a tool for main-taining critical distance became the instrument of commemoration par excellence." [5]

P.P.: Haven't you been recuperated in a way as well? Why did you feel it necessary to justify the positions presented in *The Vichy Syndrome* by writing *Vichy: An Ever-Present Past*?

H.R.: My motivation was not so much a desire to justify myself as it was a desire to put things back in their proper place. On a much more modest scale, I experienced a phenomenon similar to the one described above by Nora, a parallel which Nora himself pointed out.[6] When I wrote *The Vichy Syndrome*, I never imagined that it could be used as a tool by the growing ideology of the duty to remember, in which I, too, was submerged, like a good part of my generation. On the contrary, this book was intended to offer a historical (and thus critical) look at the evolution of the memory of Vichy in France from 1944 to the end of the 1980s, the date of its initial publication. I was not simply casting light on forgotten facts, taboos, and oversights from the postwar period and 1960s. I was also trying to focus attention on the obsessive charac-ter of these recollections in the late 1980s. I believe that this aspect of the book went largely unnoticed or, worse, was completely ignored. In-stead, the various repressions and oversights that I identified were high-lighted because this partial (in both senses of the term) reading served the growing cause of the duty to remember. For this reason, in 1994, I decided to enlist the help of Éric Conan and write *Vichy: An Ever-Present Past*, which extended my thinking on the memory of the war but also formulated a more thorough critique of the duty to remember. Conan had also been following the development of the duty to remem-ber with his articles and surveys published in the press. We both felt that we had remained true to a certain intellectual position. Looking back on it, I have the impression that we were a step ahead, judging from the fact that historians like Peter Novick defend the same arguments today. The debate is now under way internationally concerning possible excesses of the duty to remember, committed in the name of an ethics of memory and history. Moreover, whereas historians recently were critical of the failure to remember, some now denounce with equal vigor these *new* excesses, as did the polemical but rather insignificant book by Norman

5. Nora, "The Era of Commemoration," in Nora, ed., *Realms of Memory*, 3: 609.
6. Nora, "Le syndrome, son passé, son avenir." This 1995 issue of *French Historical Studies* also included articles by John Hellman and Bertram Gordon, as well as Rousso's response, "Le syndrome de l'historien."

Finkelstein, *The Holocaust Industry: Reflection on the Exploitation of Jewish Suffering*. For my own part, in *Vichy: An Ever-Present Past*, I attempted to maintain as much detachment as possible in my analysis of this obsessional residue of the past. In the intervening years, this phenomenon has become obvious to everyone—which was not at all the case when I published my first work. In *The Vichy Syndrome*, I had tried to draw attention to the problems created by the gaps existing between real events and their interpretation, in particular during the phase of repression in the 1950s and 1960s. Similarly, with *Vichy: An Ever-Present Past*, I wanted to identify the contradictions and abuses of the duty to remember, which seemed to reach a paroxysm in the early 1980s, only to be exceeded by the commotion surrounding the Papon trial in 1997–98. In other words, neither the journalist nor the historian had changed their views. Instead, it was the phenomenon itself which had changed, taking on new dimensions and importance. It developed its own brand of empty "speechification," new oversights and taboos, with these latter being almost as strong as those that France had known forty years prior, but now in the opposite direction.

P.P.: In what ways is this valorization of memory a problem?

H.R.: That our societies be attentive to conserving the past and to unearthing its most difficult aspects is not in itself a problem. On the contrary, the problem lies in the means by which memory is expressed today in the social domain and, even more important, in the objectives pursued by those who have turned memory into a value in and of itself, treating it at times as a sort of lay religion. Nietzsche wrote, "There is a degree of insomnia, of rumination, of historical awareness, which injures and finally destroys a living thing, whether a man, a people or a culture" (Nietzsche 90). As much an effect as a cause of the ideology of memory, this boiling over of our past strikes me as just as worrisome as the denial of the past. In fact, these are simply inverted symptoms of the same difficulty in accepting the reality of this past. Consequently, we are unable to confront the present or imagine the future.

There are a number of possible causes for this phenomenon (though what I will offer here are more personal intuitions than polished demonstrations). If this anguished, haunted relation to the past reveals itself in the form of a valorization of memory and not just through an increased interest in "tradition" or scholarly history, it is perhaps due to a redefinition of the contours of public space. This is particularly visible with regard to the question of minorities, be they regional or local, religious, ethnic, or sexual (especially with the emergence of women as a distinct and unique category). These groups and entities are real in some instances or the product of a new system of social representations in others. Their boundaries are accordingly more or less easy to define. For several years now, they have been calling for recognition in the public domain, from which they judge themselves, rightly or wrongly, to have been excluded. This unprecedented presence of history's marginalized groups on the public stage takes two primary forms. In addition to their political activity, these groups generally reappropriate the past in order to construct a specific history in deliberate opposition to general history (national history, for instance). In this context, these groups turn more readily to memory, that is, to popular accounts like oral records, than to scholarly history, because the problem for them lies precisely in the fact that history has (or is supposed to have) overlooked the specific roles of certain agents. In most cases, this sought-after identity must rely on more or less justified or reinvented roots in a past that legitimizes its claims. This is necessary for those who wish to claim the identity in question for themselves and for others. Consequently, these groups have a tendency to try to write their own history, outside of the usual research ranks, even if their causes have often received encouraging echoes from the academic world. The emergence of the notion of memory in the domain of the social sciences and even the rise to prominence of the history of the present are in part a consequence of this phenomenon.

P.P.: One cannot simultaneously take into account the end of the legacies produced by the Gaullists and the Communists. Nora speaks in *Realms of Memory* of a France *à la carte*. Since 1968, the past has become a coveted object for groups, local collectives, and regions. Girondist France has gotten the upper hand on Jacobin France.[7]

H.R.: Perhaps, but notice that you yourself fall back on traditional historical categories which, though justified, could also be reexamined in light of today's context. The Girondists never imagined what Europe or the "global village" might be like. In the heat of the revolutionary years, when the struggles opened up infinite possibilities (including the worst), they were looking as much to the past as to the future. But one

---

7. In the French Revolution, the Jacobins generally favored a centralized state and defended the notion of a united, indivisible republic. The Girondist tradition, on the contrary, sought political decentralization. Its partisans promoted a federalist approach that would grant more power to cities, regions, and ethnic and religious communities. For two centuries now, these traditions have continued to do battle with each other over the nature of the French state and nation. Recent French politics are seeing these debates grow increasingly heated. Trans.

cannot avoid such historical metaphors and analogies, precisely because the past continues to live within us, if only through categories of the imaginary. Moreover, it is debatable whether avoiding such historical references would be desirable.

Similarly, without being a diehard materialist, I believe that the decline of a given political legacy is not so much the *cause* of social, economic, and international changes as it is the *consequence* of changes whose scope extends far beyond it. Typically, this decline occurs when the legacy in question fails to develop a new project for itself in recognition of intervening changes. In this respect, you are quite right, although France is far from being the only country in which this phenomenon has occurred. The breakup of the national past into multiple traditions, invented or uncovered, is only the companion piece to the crisis of the Republican model. The phenomenon itself merits close analysis with regard not to its idealized form but to the actual history of the Republican model (since no political model exists independent of the litmus test of reality). The current dismay over the Republican decline obeys the same nostalgic logic as the call to revere the past that is formulated by groups (or implied by their ideas) growing out of multiculturalism and the valorization of difference.

This reservation notwithstanding, I think that the decline of the great political, national, and union traditions and their loss of relevance and appeal have contributed to the current tendency to deal with the past in terms of memory rather than history. This leads to strange reversals of what used to happen. The memory of the Holocaust now reaches outside of the circle of Jewish communities to which it was largely restricted for a long time. Its emergence into the public sphere is not without its contradictions, since the articulation of this memory wavers between a desire to see the memory recognized by international and national ensembles and a tendency to preserve it at the heart of the community itself, as a sort of cement used to solidify the group.

P.P.: Isn't this the price to be paid for the democratization of culture? Isn't this a consequence of the "Spielberg Effect," which has now even tainted the memory of the Holocaust?

H.R.: I suppose it's possible, though I am less critical of Spielberg than you. After all, one wonders whether dubious productions—even loathsome ones like the American television miniseries *Holocaust* in 1978 or the 1993 film *Schindler's List*—had an even greater effect on public opinion than the trials of figures such as Paul Touvier or Maurice Papon. Of course, neither the trials nor the movies measure up to Claude

Lanzmann's film *Shoah*, which places itself in a completely different realm. Completed in 1985, this exceptional film is as unique as the event of which it speaks, and its influence will be long term. The problem lies in the disappearance of the hierarchy that used to exist between different forms of representation of the past, as well as between the different vectors of memory mentioned above. One has the distinct impression that for the general public today a film, history book, television program, and newspaper article can all have the same pedagogical impact when it comes to speaking of the past. This form of competition is particularly fierce in the instance of contemporary history, insofar as certain subjects are now coveted by the publishing, film, and audiovisual markets. Cast in the guise of memory, the past has value. Consequently, in our society, it has retail value as well.

One can deplore or celebrate this state of affairs. However, the absence of representational hierarchy does generate a feeling of confusion and a loss of dependable reference points. The blame for this confusion is widely shared. Some historians present their claims as scholars of and militants for memory, believing their legitimacy to be equal when they pass from one domain to the other. Conversely, some militants claim to be on the same footing as historians merely for having opened a few crates of archives. It also happens that journalists and directors of documentaries flock to an already well established historical subject, announcing that "nothing has ever been done on it." Oblivious to their own ignorance, they nonetheless profit from the fact that their audience will be incomparably larger than the historian's university readership. Some historians—and I include myself in this group—operate under the illusion that they can express themselves with the same legitimacy on a television soundstage or courtroom witness stand as in a university amphitheater. Lastly, some of the agents of recent history confuse the necessity to bear witness or the occasionally real possibility of becoming a historian with the temptation to fashion a legend in their own lifetime. Today, this confusion comes just as much from the offer as from the demand, just as much from the postures adopted by those who claim to speak of the past with a certain authority as from the expectations of those who listen to or read their accounts.

The lack of an operative distinction between different levels of discourse is particularly flagrant on television. Images of the present, the immediate past, and a more distant past all flow by at the same pace and intensity, in montages that communicate a sense of urgency. In so doing, television, at least as it is conceived by the major networks, flattens or suppresses the "foreignness" of the past, creating the illusion that the past lives on by the simple fact of our projecting animated images from another time.

P.P.: History no longer manages to move beyond itself. As Jean Baudrillard is fond of saying, history implodes when caught up within our society's fixation on current events.

H.R.: I don't know whether history "implodes," but its status changes, since time on the whole is perceived differently now. We live in the age of speed, immediacy, and the instantaneous. The value of a bit of information is measured not in terms of its reliability but in terms of its rapidity or, better still, its perceived capacity to anticipate the events themselves. The public wants to know the tenor of a public decision before any deliberations take place or the result of a conflict before the war even breaks out. The very notion of duration appears to have become unbearable. Thus, the past seems to slip away, which in turn provokes the desire to bring it back into the present, to reinvest it in current issues, rather than observing it where it belongs, from where we belong. We can now see why memory seems more valuable than history. History is an approach that puts the past at a distance; it is an effort destined to re-create and help us understand the weight and complexity of past events. As we have already noted, memory is a faculty that brings the past into the present. It is characterized by an affective, emotional relation to the past that ignores the hierarchies of time and abolishes distance.

In a certain sense, the current valorization of memory, or at least of certain acts and discourses which claim to speak in the name of memory, ends up achieving the opposite result of that intended. This valorization impedes a real apprenticeship of the past, of duration, of the passage of time. By the same token, it also weighs on our ability to imagine the future. We live in the age of the "imaginary" where the symbolic— understood here as a perception of self and of the collectivity situated in a universe limited by time and space—has lost its value as a structuring force.

P.P.: In a recent article, Zaki Laïdi wrote, "Paul Ricœur has said that the greatest utopia were those which managed to seize upon the as-yet unaccomplished in a society's traditions and that this unrealized element constituted a reserve stock of meaning. However, in commemorating the past, one moves away from this approach to the extent that one identifies the past with a golden age. Since we wish to return to it, this presupposes its prior accomplishment, but we wish to return to it without 'modernizing' it. Moreover, as soon as one considers socioeconomic problems, the solutions of the past are of no use, as shown by the debate on globalization. Similarly, the future seems too unpromising for any temporal investment in the future. We then find ourselves cut off from the past, yet unable to attach ourselves to a future. Pierre Nora recently noted that one would have to go all the way back to the last days of the Roman Empire to find a comparable situation." Do you agree?

H.R.: Yes, with one exception. I believe that our societies can no longer formulate representations of historical continuity. They live in a crisis of the future, that is to say, in a mode where they find it difficult to think of the future in reassuring terms or even to imagine it at all. Postmodern jargon aside, it is easy to see today that the retrospective is more valued than the prospective. This backward glance, however, is more commonly cast on the recent past, source of anxious questions, than on the distant and completed past. When the latter surfaces, it is more as an object of entertainment and folkloric curiosity than as a source of inspiration. It suffices to recall the palinodes surrounding the 1,500th anniversary of Clovis's baptism. In light of such phenomena, one gets the impression that time — understood here in the sense of "historical becoming" — has shrunk substantially. We are not able to cast our gaze very far before us, toward an ever more uncertain future, nor very far behind us, toward the quite recent past.

I must add one important objection, however. Admittedly, one frequently encounters a nostalgia for a golden age long past whose distant fire still shines brightly in our minds, particularly in contrast with the spectacle of our current "decadence." In my opinion, religiously invoking the "secular and Republican model" is an example of this. But most important we must recognize that the past which haunts us is not a golden age but rather an iron age, one of fire and blood. The memory of Auschwitz is indisputably the principal cause of the dawning of the age of memory.

P.P.: In *L'histoire déchirée*, Enzo Traverso writes, "To think about Auschwitz is to try to understand — despite the arrogance [of such a gesture] and aporia of reason — outside of the official commemorations and beyond the dogmatic taboos. One must try to understand in order to reintroduce a moral dimension to history, to not forget those who perished and, lastly, to learn, in the words of Ernst Bloch, 'the upright progress of humanity.' "[8] Is it impossible to understand Auschwitz?

---

8. Traverso, *L'histoire déchirée: essai sur Auschwitz et les intellectuels* (Paris: Éditions du Cerf, 1997) 236. An English-language translation is forthcoming. Trans.

H.R.: I don't know. Moreover, who could answer this question? Like Enzo Traverso, however, I am convinced that one must try. The obstacles to understanding are considerable on a number of counts, as much for the history as for the memory of this event. The uniqueness of this historical event has been followed by the uniqueness of its remembrance. The burden we still feel today, marked by the continual reexamination of this past, is proportional to the silences, incomprehension, and even denial that followed the discovery of the Nazi crimes. Inconsolable memory is commensurate with lived or inflicted trauma. How many generations will it take before we can assign these events an "acceptable" place in history without our conscience breaking into a cold sweat? How long before we can close the books on them? Yet another question that must go unanswered.

In this respect, however, it is useful to remember that memory as an approach to the past is a cornerstone of Jewish tradition. Yosef Hayim Yerushalmi's insights are unsurpassed on this subject. Almost twenty years ago now (see *Zakhor: Jewish History and Jewish Memory*), he was one of the first to rediscover the importance of Halbwachs's notion of collective memory. Yerushalmi has shown that history—scholarly, detached accounts of the past—has never played a preeminent role in Jewish culture or in the transmission of Jewish heritage from one generation to another. It has always taken a backseat to collective memory. Even the Shoah and the creation of the state of Israel have not significantly modified this tradition, although in Jewish communities today the central conflicts between memory and history are more contentious than in the past. It can be argued, from a factual point of view as well as from a moral one, that the current situation is poetic justice, a bit like a vengeance exacted on history: As a result of the universal valorization of memory and of the memory of Auschwitz, Jewish tradition now exerts a strong influence in a world in which that tradition was very nearly erased.

P.P.: And yet you are critical of this particular instance of poetic justice.

H.R.: Yes, because an acculturation of this sort, however justified it may be on a moral level, can only be taken so far. The memory of the Holocaust, not in and of itself but rather the manner in which it is understood and kept alive today, cannot become a new form of religiosity without major risks. First—but I mention it only to dismiss it—there is the risk of anti-Semitic reactions. This risk should not be heeded, because any behavior attributed to the Jews, be it real or imagined, is an inexhaustible source of anti-Semitism. In my opinion, a much more serious risk is in a continual affirmation of the Holocaust's singularity (with respect to the past, of course, because no one can speak for the future). The result can be the transformation of this singularity into a dogma that encourages its holders to deny any possibility of comparison between the Holocaust and the other mass slaughters of this century. The Holocaust would thus lose its exemplarity.

Yet another danger is that of having Jews represented in the cultural imaginary solely as victims, especially if this "religion" is practiced not by actual survivors of the tragedy but by their descendants. While in the case of the former their defense of the memory of the Holocaust is entirely legitimate, in the case of the latter, this memory, when it is maintained with fervor, amounts more to a quest for identity than an inscription of the Holocaust in a historical "becoming."

I make these remarks with a full awareness of the issues involved. Jewish identity cannot be eternally rooted in the suffering of an older generation, a generation which will soon become ancestral. Sooner or later, Jewish identity must have a new project that points it toward the future, giving it an active, forward-looking content. After all, the state of Israel is in large part built against this image of the Jew as victim. Contrary to what is commonly thought, it is not until the Eichmann trial in 1961 that the young Jewish state sees the return of memory and an increased awareness of what the tragedy had been. In fact, one must wait a few more years before the memory of the Holocaust becomes a central topic in public debate. In Israel, it is only with the series of crises in the 1970s that the Holocaust enters the political imaginary as an active element, a phenomenon which had already occurred in other countries.[9] The Hebrew state was therefore not founded on victimization. On the contrary, it was based on a project, albeit debatable and today superseded. Initially, this project depended partly on forgetting, as is the case with most of the Jewish communities of the Diaspora. Not many people realize that, rightly or wrongly, the duty to remember is an attitude that was not uniformly shared by survivors after the war—far from it, in fact. This was particularly true in France where the desire to reestablish the national community, sometimes even by force or constraint, was a widespread, if not dominant, sentiment.

9. A recent current of Israeli historiographical thought has dedicated its efforts to demonstrating this chronology; see, e.g., Tom Segev, *The Seventh Million: The Israelis and the Holocaust*.

I am not claiming here that we should return to this prior state, which of course would make no sense. However, I do believe that it is necessary to invent a means of affirming and incorporating a Jewishness that is grounded in the issues of our time and not solely in the memory of the Holocaust. This is as relevant for Jews as it is for others.

P.P.: In your opinion, what are the more general consequences of the uniqueness of the memory of the Shoah?

H.R.: It is henceforth evident that the difficult, if not impossible, management of this past has had consequences on the perception of historical time itself and on how people think of and about history. Contrary to the analyses of Maurice Halbwachs, who back in the 1930s was thinking through human history on a large scale without being able to imagine what his fate would be in the near future, in recent years memory has not been able to fulfill its traditional role, which is to preserve the identity of groups and individuals. The rupture provoked by the unprecedented event of the Holocaust has been and probably will remain insurmountable. At the very most, collective memory can liberate a voice, organize it, put it into circulation, and thus see to it that the suffering and responsibilities for this event are more widely shared within the community. As I see it, this is the sole purpose served by trials for crimes against humanity, as long as one does not consider the courtroom to be the only place where these voices can be heard. But collective memory cannot do any more than this, at least if one judges by what has happened over the last thirty years, the period during which the memory of the Holocaust has become so prominent.

That said, one cannot surrender to the claim that it is impossible to gain and transmit knowledge about this event, particularly if one is a historian. Asserting in a repetitive and mechanical manner that the event belongs to the domain of the indescribable is to fall back into the register of faith or, worse still, offer an unconscious alibi for not listening. It is useless to ignore everything that has been said, written, and filmed over the last fifty years and claim that all rational, historical, and critical approaches to this event are bound to fail (or can be considered criminal, since they risk rendering the event banal). The Holocaust was committed by humans; it can be explained by humans—even if the explanation will undoubtedly fall short of the reality of the event. Moreover, who could claim, aside perhaps from direct survivors, to be able to judge what an adequate representation of these events would be? Despite the aporia that may crop up in such an effort, history has the obligation to try to explain.

P.P.: What about the duty to remember? What becomes of it?

H.R.: There is a gap, a gulf even, between memory as an ethical necessity and the duty to remember such as it is practiced today. Originally articulated by Primo Levi and others, the injunction of the duty to remember was inscribed in the continuity of the event. It was a call to survivors to testify, to bear witness—not simply to pass on as much as possible of their experience but also to fight against the fear of not being heard. Even more important, it was a call to resist their own temptation to forget, a temptation which is at work in memory when one tries to recover the thread of a continuity so radically ruptured. Describing his meeting with Allied officers on April 12, 1945, the day after the liberation of the Buchenwald camp, Jorge Semprun wrote,

> You can tell all about this experience. You have merely to think about it. And set to it. And have the time, of course, and the courage, for a boundless and probably never-ending account, illuminated (as well as enclosed, naturally) by that possibility of going on forever. Even if you wind up repeating yourself. Even if you remain caught up in it, prolonging death, if necessary—revising it endlessly in the nooks and crannies of the story. Even if you become no more than the language of this death, and live at its expense, fatally.
> But can people hear everything, imagine everything? Will they be able to understand? Will they have the necessary patience, passion, compassion, and fortitude? I begin to doubt it, in that first moment, that first meeting with men from *before*, from the *outside*, emissaries from life—when I see the stunned, almost hostile, and certainly suspicious look in the eyes of the three officers. (Semprun 14)

At its origin, this was an injunction that a survivor might address to him- or herself, in order not to forget, in order not to forget him- or herself. Today, however, the duty to remember has changed into an injunction that the younger generations—those not having lived the events in question—peremptorily address to their contemporaries, sometimes forgetting that among those contemporaries there are people who did in fact live those tragic years, even if it was under other circumstances than those who were persecuted. On one of the countless television programs devoted to the duty to remember, for instance, I remember seeing a teenager who had just entered high school explain that she was going to "pass on the memory of Auschwitz" to the children she planned to have one day.

When the duty to remember takes the form of undertakings such as Serge Klarsfeld's *Mémorial de la déportation des juifs de France*, or his *Mémorial des enfants juifs*, it fulfills its proper function: It ensures the remembrance of the dead, which restores their identity and offers them a symbolic grave materialized by their name. This is essential in ancestral Jewish tradition. However, when the duty to remember is turned into a moral code and sets out to impose a permanent, "imprescriptible" consciousness of the crime as a doctrine of sorts, then it finds itself at an impasse. You cannot force an entire society to remain eternally riveted on the past, however tragic it may be, just as you cannot recklessly and indiscriminately shackle society with full responsibility for the crimes committed. This is all the more evident when the means used to maintain the duty to remember no longer has much to do at all with morality. It is problematic, for instance, when the duty to remember becomes an agitprop that one brandishes provocatively, showing a brazen disdain for the justice that one had previously clamored for. We can respect without any reservations Serge Klarsfeld's work as a historian and as a militant for memory (in the noblest sense of the term). On the other hand, we can question whether he has the right to believe himself above the law and common morality, as he and his son gave the impression during the Papon trial. They exerted great pressure on the magistrates, they made personal attacks on the presiding judge, and they manipulated the media at the expense of the justice system, all the while knowing that no one would dare contradict them.

P.P.: Are morality and history really so incompatible?

H.R.: Moralism does not mix well with historical truth. In order to maintain its edifying power, it ends up cutting corners with the facts and slipping into a narrative divorced from reality. It suffices to read certain reputedly serious daily papers to see how they have made the duty to remember into a regularly featured column or editorial theme. On their front pages, they repeatedly publish approximations, inaccuracies, or even factual contradictions, often doing so with the arrogance of those who have taken on the mantle of doling out civic and moral lessons to the general public. Historians certainly are not immune to such lapses in judgment either. However, what is troubling here is not so much the unreliable nature of the information or the absence of factual verification (a shortcoming widely shared today). Rather, these errors grow out of a vigilance that has been raised to the level of an ideology and that does not shy away from occasionally using misinformation to keep the public mobilized. We have seen examples of this in newspaper campaigns led against intellectuals or scholars as soon as the latter adopt critical stances with respect to the duty to remember. It is an old reflex among some intellectuals on the Left, a carry-over from the Stalinist period: They seek to silence any opinion that strays from the party line under the pretext that defending the "cause" requires suppressing all internal dissonance. In the long run, this attitude ends up weakening the intended objective and turns the duty to remember into a sectarian struggle, which is contrary to the imperative to tell the truth that Primo Levi made a priority in the original duty to remember.

P.P.: What about the problem of reparations?

H.R.: This is the fundamental problem. When we attempt, fifty years after the fact, in the name of the duty to remember, to redress wrongs that were not resolved right after the war, or when we institute a judicial concept like imprescriptibility, we create a paradox that is difficult to overcome, especially if we assert at the same time that the crimes committed during the Holocaust are irreparable. Calling for moral, symbolic, material, or judicial reparation after the heat of the moment implies that debts always have their price. Once paid, the debt should be settled, so that one can henceforth speak of forgetting, forgiving, or simply turning the page. In this instance, though, this option seems unacceptable and is probably impossible. One makes a legitimate call for reparation, all the while proclaiming that the crime is irreparable. From the moment the partisans of the duty to remember refuse to choose between the two possibilities, they back themselves into a corner. The notion of imprescriptibility has been transformed from a judicial term with a precise meaning—the possibility of bringing a criminal to justice as long as he or she lives—into a moral one, applicable to times and places that no longer have clear limits or markers. Imprescriptibility has led to the creation of an inexhaustible debt—an "imprescriptible" debt, to quote French president Jacques Chirac from his July 16, 1995, speech.[10] And yet at the same time Chirac conveyed the impression that the debt could be resolved. The desire to keep the issue alive has necessitated an endless increase in the ante. The entire process seems to have taken on a life of its own. After the Paul Touvier trial, the Maurice Papon trial comes to the fore; after Papon, why not flush out and charge another of the Vichy administrators still alive today, as some people demanded before the Bordeaux verdict was even given? Similarly, after inaugurating the July 16 commemoration—a first in French history, since it marks the memory of a state crime, that of the Vel' d'hiv' roundup[11]—

10. See "Chirac Affirms France's Guilt in Fate of Jews." Trans.

11. On July 16, 1942, French police arrested 13,000 Jewish men, women, and children. The prisoners were held initially in the Vélodrome d'hiver (or Vel' d'hiv') before being interned in the Parisian suburb of Drancy and later deported to German-run camps. Trans.

Chirac gave a speech discussing the responsibilities of Vichy and of France for events occurring during the war. Following this long-awaited presidential gesture comes the request for compensation for the confiscated belongings of French Jews and so on.

P.P.: This request is perhaps impossible to fulfill, but it is nonetheless legitimate.

H.R.: These are two different things. The process I am describing strikes me as vain and even risky, insofar as it continues to attribute to Jewish memory an ever-more separate and distinct place in the French national memory. The most striking illustration of this was given in the government's handling of the various files compiled under Vichy to tabulate and monitor the Jewish population. Chirac, president of the French Republic, decided to turn them over to the Center for Contemporary Jewish Documentation (Centre de Documentation Juive Contemporaine), a *private* organization. This affair sparked a vast polemic and brought the paradox to its peak: The duty to remember had quite rightly insisted that the history of Vichy, with its crimes and evil deeds, must be unflinchingly incorporated into France's national history and memory, yet here an entire domain of the documentation that would assist such an effort was in a sense "privatized," as if the memory of this crime concerned only the Jewish community and not the nation as a whole.

In the long run, I think it preferable to concentrate on the means, rituals, and forms of transmission of the past that allow us to live *with* the memory of the tragedy rather than trying to live *without* it (as in the years right after the war) or *against* it (as we do today). History can then play its role of distancing these events while trying to be less impacted by political, community, and identity issues which cloak themselves in the duty to remember. Sooner or later, the "age of memory" will give way to the "age of history," and we will then need to come up with new ways to attend to our memories.

Chapter 2
For a History of the Present

Philippe Petit: Before we move on to the origins of the "history of the present" and of the Institute of the History of the Present, I would like to discuss the problem of periodization in history. Victor Duruy, historian and minister of education under Napoleon, was the first to introduce contemporary history into secondary school education. What difference is there between Duruy's program and the "history of the present," the phrase which figures so prominently in the name of the institute that you currently direct?

Henry Rousso: In a French tradition dating back to the nineteenth century, contemporary history begins with the French Revolution. The history of the present deals with the recent past, the one for which there are still living actors. But before turning to an explanation of what the history of the present is, one needs to keep in mind that the notion of "contemporaneity" is as old and as problematic as the discipline of history itself. It is even one of its principal constitutive elements, on two grounds in particular. First, all history is "contemporary," to borrow from Benedetto Croce's famous phrase. Like everyone else, historians can only speak of the past in the present. They reconstitute discourses and actions from the past with concepts, preoccupations, and vocabularies which are those of their time. Addressing their accounts to their contemporaries, they attempt to restore a truth from the past as accurately as possible. They try to establish this truth by assembling documents and building them into proofs. They work from an inevitably anachronistic position, even if the craft of history consists of overcoming this natural obstacle. Historians must not attribute to agents of another era intentions that those people could not possibly have had in their time; conversely, they should also avoid explaining historical events in light of what happened afterwards. Along similar lines, they must resist the

distorting effects of the "retrospective illusion": An event is not in-
eluctable simply because it ended up occurring. Historians must be conscious, too, that they may never be certain of uncovering the original
spirit and meaning of past words or actions. Their work is inscribed
within a dialectic, a tension between the words of the past and those of
the present.

Because it raises one of the principal problems facing historians, this
elementary truth should remain present in the minds of all scholars
seeking to define the notion of "contemporaneity." One is constantly
confronted with the alterity and heterogeneity that the passage of time
produces, and this can be true of even very short periods of time. On
the one hand, we are estranged from our own history because the apparent continuity that an individual or group owes to the work of memory cannot entirely counterbalance the real and significant changes that
the passage of time brings about. This is one of the major stumbling
blocks for the history of the present, though by the same token it is also
the justification for its existence as a distinct historiographical domain.
We must resist thinking that the proximity of the periods or phenomena
studied can dispense with this otherness. We cannot forget that the past
remains a land at once foreign and familiar. At the same time, however,
this otherness is the very reason that historians study recent or even
current periods. The historical project consists precisely in describing,
explaining, and situating alterity, in putting it at a distance.

P.P.: And on the other hand?

H.R.: On the other hand, the historical study of the recent past goes
back to the origins of history as an intellectual approach. Herodotus's
History or Thucydides' *Peloponnesian War* are in part "histories of the
present," with all due respect for the anachronism of the concept. More
recently, contemporary history was institutionalized during the nineteenth century and has been a productive field in historical studies ever
since. In the wake of World War I, Pierre Renouvin developed a new
historical school in France that focused on international relations. No
longer understood as the study of treaties, charters, and the ties between powers (as the old diplomatic history had done), *relations* was
now taken in the broadest sense of the term, allowing for the study of
the economic, cultural, and political interactions between nations. Renouvin and his disciples were sought out by official sources in the 1920s
and asked to draw up as rigorous and objective an account as possible
that would establish Imperial Germany's responsibility in triggering the
war. This is a remarkable precedent in the history of the present. A group

of historians were faced with the difficulty of understanding a dramatic event that was still a burning issue, doubled by the challenge of satisfying a social and political request laden with substantial stakes. Between the two world wars, one can also note that contemporary history was practiced both by the positivists and by their opponents at *Annales*, even though at that time neither group recognized it as being entirely legitimate from a scientific point of view. In *Histoire de la nation française: essai d'une histoire de l'évolution du peuple français*, first published in 1933 but extended through a series of new editions going up to 1939, Charles Seignobos spends only three pages (out of more than four hundred) on the consequences of World War I. An emblematic figure of the positivist current, Seignobos concludes that in the 1920s and 1930s (that is, during what was the present for the author), "The French people have begun to appear as they really are: prudent, reasonable and peace-loving" (Seignobos 394). Formulated on the eve of World War II, this diagnosis demonstrates the interest but also the limits of an interpretation made in the heat of the moment, in which historians are immersed in events every bit as much as their fellow citizens. Similarly, in *Strange Defeat*, a work written between July and September 1940, Marc Bloch proves to be a dazzlingly lucid historian of the present. He presents himself as a historian, that is to say, as a scholar armed with a critical method, committed to studying life and thus to dispelling the illusion that the past is dead. At the same time, though, he also appears in the work as an eyewitness talking about his experiences and examining his own era. In the end, however, the exceptional quality of this work owes more to the tragic context and Bloch's personal talent than to the methods associated with *Annales*, the journal which Bloch and Lucien Febvre founded in 1929.

P.P.: Bloch's brilliant insights are clearly tied to the context of the period, but they are also the result of a certain way of understanding history, the product of years of reflection on French society. Bloch felt that the present is unintelligible without knowledge of the past, but he did not believe that knowledge about the present is in itself a mirage. Isn't it the role of the historian to formulate in the present the lessons of history?

H.R.: Marc Bloch speaks of a dialectic between the past and the present as the founding tension driving the craft of the historian. In this respect, his most original contribution is not so much in reminding us that the present cannot be understood without studying the past—this, after all, is the essence of all historical knowledge. Rather, it is to show us that the opposite is equally true: Analysis of the present allows us to understand the past. Bloch is by no means a captive of the teleological effect whereby only the end, known after the fact, provides the meaning of an event. But he does defend the idea, rather original in his day, that the personal experience of historians—as individuals, citizens, and intellectuals living through the tragedies of history (as Bloch did himself)—constitutes a significant asset in their attempts to explain the past. Direct experience of both world wars, for example, has been a decisive element in approaching the war and military activities as historical phenomena. Had Bloch not been assassinated by the Nazis, he probably would have written other important books in his area of specialization (medieval history) as well as in contemporary history ("history of the present").

For me, this vision of the craft of history amounts to a liberating type of thinking, because it rejects the idea that people or societies are conditioned or determined by their past without any possibility of escaping it. On the contrary, in examining history, people seek to compare their own experiences with those of the generations that preceded them, in an exchange that remains open, free, and undetermined.

P.P.: Does Marc Bloch's work remain a source of inspiration for historians of the present?

H.R.: Yes, of course. But what I wanted to point out was the extent to which certain great twentieth-century medievalist or modernist historians, who in their professional activities usually expressed (at best) general indifference or (at worst) suspicion or even hostility toward the practice of contemporary history as its own distinct, scientific discipline, were upon occasion led to cast, consciously or not, through their direct contact with individuals and citizens, a historical glance on their own era. At times it was a glance of unequaled lucidity. The *Annales* school was in part built against the imperialism, real or imagined, of the scholarly tradition of political and event history. This strategy of marking itself off from other approaches allowed it to promote a history of long duration, a structural history grounded in the analysis of economic and social phenomena. However, this innovative and ambitious approach, which won the French school an international audience, came together as a result of a major rupture in history (World War II), in a century brutally marked by a series of momentous, tragic, and deadly events (such as the Holocaust) that in some ways exceed the limits of human comprehension. This method has shown a lack of interest in events, politics, and contingency in an era that has seen one world war follow another, two great economic crises, at least one revolution of planetary repercussions, and the arrival of new forms of tyranny (Nazism, fascism, and full-fledged communist governments). This apparent contradiction raises questions about the limits of this approach and about the academic milieu, whose members are not always able to gauge properly the upheaval that they live through in the company of their fellow citizens. Sooner or later, historians had to turn their attention to producing a history of the politics and events—two of this century's dominant traits—in order to respond to the challenges this century poses to history and to the social sciences in general.

P.P.: Are you saying that the history of the present was a bit frowned upon by the academic world and some of its most prestigious representatives?

H.R.: In academic circles, this historical approach was regarded with suspicion even into the 1970s. In the 1950s, René Rémond was already calling energetically for the development of a history of the recent past. He mostly had in mind the interwar period, with the 1930s being of particular interest to him. Twenty years later, the situation had changed somewhat, particularly on the fringes of the university milieu, as in the case of the National Foundation of Political Science (Fondation Nationale des Sciences Politiques, or FNSP).[1] But the old biases were still holding strong. In 1975, when I chose to do my master's thesis on the history of Vichy, I had the distinct impression of a certain reticence on the part of some of my teachers, although they were hardly conservatives. It was as if this choice were potentially harmful to my fledgling academic career, both because the project consisted of research on contemporary history and because Vichy was still a delicate subject. People often informed me that trying to do the history of the twentieth century was "at best political science, at worst journalism." If one compares it with the situation today, the field of contemporary history was still considered historiography's poor cousin barely twenty-five years ago. There were very few historians of contemporary history who had any reputation outside the circle of specialists, in comparison with those working on Antiquity, the Middle Ages, or the modern period (fifteenth to

1. Created in 1945 as part of a series of reforms in French higher education, the FNSP picks up where the Free School of Political Science (École Libre des Sciences Politiques) left off: It allows the government to maintain a directing role in training France's future political elite. Among its scholarly endeavors, the FNSP oversees the Institute of Studies on Politics (Institut d'Études Politiques) as well as numerous research groups in political sociology, economics, international relations, history, etc. Trans.

eighteenth centuries), who were the most highly regarded in the profession, along with the "new historians." In this respect, the latter merely preceded the historians of the present who now are having their turn—though for other reasons—in the media spotlight. This relative marginality was consistent with a certain long-term tendency. What is new today is the current popularity of the history of the present, with this historiographical approach being not only recognized as legitimate (independently of the intrinsic quality of its production, which is varied, as with any scientific domain) but also very much in demand.

P.P.: I sense some reticence on your part.

H.R.: Traditionally, and especially since the nineteenth century, three types of objection have been (and continue to be) formulated against contemporary history. First, this type of historiography lacks the necessary temporal distance and violates one of historiography's fundamental axioms, which argues that only completed events can be the object of historical knowledge. Second, this form of historiography is more likely than other approaches to be the victim of personal passions and gives rise to ideological conflicts. Third—and this is the most severe of the critiques—this sort of historiography is quite simply impossible to perform for practical reasons, since the relevant archives are not available for consultation.

"Completed events present themselves to us with a much greater clarity than those which are in the midst of unfolding," wrote Denis Fustel de Coulanges (Bédarida 76). In *Dimensions de la conscience historique*, Raymond Aron, who fortunately did not always apply his axioms to his own work, formulates this postulate even more sharply: "The object of study in history is a reality which has ceased to be" (100–101). This first objection raises a fundamental problem that has traditionally confronted scholars of contemporary history, for it means that there should be a waiting period during which any investigation of the past would be ill advised. We are supposed to let time run its course. In other words, the historian should not appear on the scene until after the period of forgetting, once the dead are good and buried. In this extremely traditional conception of the discipline, the proper time for history could be seen as the inverse of the proper time for justice. (I will say more about this comparison later.) While the law decrees that one cannot prosecute or punish *after the expiration* of various amounts of time (with the notable exception of the imprescriptible crime against humanity), the historian supposedly should only begin work *starting with* the completion of a certain waiting period, which, as a matter of fact, no one has ever precisely defined. Only the lawmakers have ruled on the matter, having legislated time periods concerning access to public archives.

P.P.: What should the normal waiting period be? How much time needs to pass before an event becomes intelligible?

H.R.: From a scientific point of view, there is no reason whatsoever to impose a delay. One of the founding principles of the "new history" was that there are an infinite number of historical objects to be studied. As soon as a historian accepts the idea that there are no boundaries hemming in historical inquiry, there is no need to set temporal boundaries either. But this is more to beg the question than to propose an argument. In truth, this position is founded on the idea that it is impossible to establish a priori from what moment a phenomenon becomes intelligible and accessible to historical knowledge. Was the French Revolution more intelligible a century later, in the 1880s, than it had been when its ashes were still warm—under the Restoration, for instance, barely twenty years later? For political reasons, in the last third of the nineteenth century, memory and to an even greater extent the revolutionary tradition both returned to occupy the forefront of the public stage. This was during the period that laid down the intellectual and then the institutional foundations for the republic. Were the hundred years that had passed a sufficient lapse at that moment, or was the residual presence of the French Revolution in the political arena an obstacle to obtaining the necessary intellectual detachment?

Another useful example is the history of communism. Clearly, this can be written with greater lucidity and reliability after the fall of the Berlin Wall and the end of the Soviet system. Not only are historians working with a mass of previously unavailable archives, but the end of the Soviet system also invites us to rethink the historical sequence inaugurated by the revolution of 1917, insofar as we are now studying a phenomenon whose "end" is known to us. We know that the system was "mortal" and that, in the end, with respect to the long duration, it had a relatively brief history, contrary to what people might have thought before 1989–91. In other words, this history appears easier to write because the event has closure, at least provisionally. But that does not mean that everything written by historians and other specialists before the Berlin Wall came down, that is, while the event was still unfolding, was useless. And one should especially avoid assuming that it was without value. This would mean that we should have waited until the 1990s to undertake the first histories of the USSR and of the international communist system. Moreover, the history being written today, based on archives, is no more serene than that which was being written while the event was still open to a number of possible futures. Just the opposite is true. In France today, as soon as a work compares Nazism and communism, the battle lines are drawn anew, regardless of whether the book in question makes the comparison in an appropriate manner or, as in the case of the introduction to *The Black Book of Communism* (Courtois et al.), in a caricaturing one. (I will say more later about this latter point.) Whatever the conclusions this practice may produce, one should not forget that the principle of comparability is quite old. It reached its peak in the 1950s, most notably in Hannah Arendt's work on totalitarianism. One could also argue that it is perfectly legitimate on an intellectual and scientific level, even in those cases where one believes that the two systems are not equivalent, since this statement necessarily implies a prior comparison. In this respect, one can see a form of regression in today's debates, which shows that the distance or "closure" of the event does not at all attenuate the emotional and ideological charge in which the writing of history finds itself entangled.

One final example to be considered here is the history of the Occupation. Having been caught up in it for a long time now, I know that it is no easier to work on it today, nearly sixty years after the defeat in 1940, than it was ten or so years ago. The sensitivity surrounding memories of this period has not diminished with time; rather, as new generations become aware of it, the polemical nature of these debates only grows. The greater this sensitivity, the harder historical research becomes. It is true that it is much easier today than in the 1960s, when this period was still the object of official silences. But the difficulty has not decreased in a clear, even manner. It has oscillated over time, depending on the history of the memory of the event.

To put it another way, I think that the major objection to the history of the present—its lack of distance—is irrelevant. The waiting period is usually nothing more than an ideological pretext that varies according to the nature of the information requested. Every generation examines its past, distant and near, with its own categories, with different expectations, and, unless one believes that there exists a yardstick for measuring history, with a degree of pertinence that is very difficult to evaluate. This does not mean that there is no progress in historical knowledge or that all accounts are relative—in this case, to time itself. But this leads us to try to distinguish between the elements that add to cumulative knowledge and those that contribute more to the questions asked and interpretations offered. In the case of the latter, they usually bear the mark of their era and are inscribed within a given context, but even these can prove to be of interest over time.

P.P.: In your opinion, what are the reasons for the waiting periods?

H.R.: The argument is often of an ideological nature, but there is more to it than that. It is also based on the popular, seemingly self-evident notion that one must wait until the protagonists are deceased. The proper time for history would thus coincide with the time of mourning; it would begin with the time of the dead. The argument has some validity, but it is anchored more in ethical concerns than in scientific ones. Clearly, it is sometimes difficult morally to write a history in the presence of its living actors. This can bring on reflexes of self-censorship or a tendency toward indiscretions and even inquisitorial demeanors. And yet the history of the present has constituted itself as a discipline precisely because it was necessary to tackle this challenge. Following the example of most of the other social sciences that work on contemporary phenomena, it posits the working hypothesis that the presence of living actors and witnesses is in fact very much a resource. Having emerged during the 1970s, the history of the present is in this sense a product of its day, an era which has built up memory into an essential value.

P.P.: Having risen to this challenge, are you suggesting that the project of founding the history of the present was not an easy one? Did you experience a lot of difficulty in winning acceptance for the idea of history compiled in part from living witnesses?

H.R.: Exactly. The history of the present was not constituted in a defensive manner, with its practitioners excusing themselves for having to work with living witnesses or probing still open wounds. It was founded by turning the objections which have always been held against it back against themselves. It was rooted in an affirmation, the expression of the necessity of doing this kind of history, and in a refusal to allow journalists, columnists, or the other social sciences to monopolize it. By definition, the history of the present is the history of a past which is not yet dead, which is still borne in the speech and experience of living individuals, and thus, as we have seen earlier, a past consisting of active and uniquely vital memories. Of course, like all historical narratives, this type of history remains a dialogue between the living and the dead, but it is also based on a dialogue among the living, between contemporaries, about a past which is not yet entirely past but which is no longer completely current. It explores the indeterminate boundary that separates the past from the present, as do all the other forms of historical inquiry, but this approach has made it its principal object of study.

P.P.: Doesn't the history of the present contribute to a sort of acceleration of history? Isn't it vulnerable to the whims of passion by the very fact of its lack of temporal remove?

H.R.: I don't think so. I would even say that it is indispensable precisely in order to give a certain intelligibility to the phenomenon of acceleration that you mention. This acceleration and the public passions exist regardless, independently of scholarly histories of the recent past, as we just saw with the questions concerning memory. In this respect, the history of the present encounters difficulties which are proper to it but which it did not create (unless one credits historians with a power of influence that they do not really have). In truth, as we saw in the case of the supposed necessity of a waiting period, the reproach that this type of historiography is hostage to ideological conflicts is not very well founded. Any discourse having to do with history, particularly national history, is loaded with passion. In fact, the most important aspect of historical inquiry is to examine the experience of the ancients while making others aware that the quarrels and issues of the present are rooted in a certain duration and are sometimes perpetuated in other contexts. Today's debates about Vichy, which in my view have less to do with the events themselves than with how to perpetuate their memory, are neither more nor less ideological than those, still very much alive, that deal with the French Revolution. The animated—or occasionally outright hostile—tone that characterizes some of the debates over the near or distant past is not in itself an obstacle to the advancement of knowledge. These debates are a constitutive element of it, though this can of course cause us to lose ground in our knowledge—in cases, for instance, where there is a tendency toward anachronism or sterile polemics. But they can also help renew certain lines of questioning.

The real problem here is that of the political and social uses of the past. We all realize that there is no such thing as a disinterested history. History is always performed within contexts and in light of debates that historians do not control but of which they must be fully aware.

P.P.: Is the lack of archives another obstacle?

H.R.: This objection is of a different order. We can start by pointing out that this objection stems from an archaic understanding both of the historian's craft and of the notion of archive itself. It is based on the implicit supposition that archives are necessarily government archives that remain confidential for decades until the day when they are finally opened, at which point they are expected to reveal state secrets, among which will be the keys to understanding the era in question. That said, the difficulty of gaining access to public archives remains a problem for the history of the present. But historians are now getting around it by making use of other sources, beginning with testimonials from those still alive, animated and still images (photography, television, cinema, video), the recorded word (most notably radio), the press, government materials (reports, documents, and studies), privates archives, and so on. As all historians of the twentieth century know, the principal difficulty facing the historian is not the poverty of sources but their abundance and heterogeneity. One of the essential traits of this century is its production of an immeasurable number of lasting traces—at least as many as all of prior history.

P.P.: Have audiovisual media and other new techniques changed the craft of the historian, for instance, in the historian's work with witnesses?

H.R.: From the moment that it became possible to record and conserve testimonials, the entire oral tradition entered a new phase because it was no longer reserved to the relatively closed circles of family, profession, or region. Oral testimony could now find a much larger audience and participate in the foundation or preservation of a more extensive collective memory. Ethnologists, anthropologists, and sociologists realized this well before historians did. Another novelty lies in the desire to collect a truly significant number of eyewitness accounts for archival purposes, an example being what has been happening for years now with the history of the Holocaust. The fear that survivors might disappear before they had the opportunity to speak generated a considerable quantity of testimonials—beginning in 1945 itself and not just recently, as is too often suggested. Of all different types in all variety of media, they constitute a resource without equivalent in history.

There are some important distinctions to make here, however. An eyewitness's account is not necessarily oral, and numerous traditional archives that have been used for centuries by historians (police interrogations, for example) are simply testimonials transcribed onto paper, which symbolically gives them additional prestige but does not take away any of their testimonial character. Along the same lines, it is possible in the future that audiovisual testimony will be preferred to written forms, due to the contact with the witness's voice and image that the former provides. One should also distinguish between oral sources, oral archives, and oral histories. By oral sources, I mean testimony solicited by the historian, employed in the framework of a specific research project, and integrated and compared with other sources. In the case of oral archives, one is dealing with vast corpora of testimony that are recorded in a systematic manner without necessarily being directed toward a particular research goal. For this reason, they can easily be used later in a number of ways. Finally, oral history is much more than a mere technique. Born for the most part among Anglo-Saxon scholars, this historiographical current privileges the words of history's excluded (real or hypothetical), to counter the archives left behind by the elite or those in power.[2]

The choice of terminology is not insignificant, of course. In avoiding the use of the term *oral history*, as we have done for years at the IHTP, we mark a refusal to grant testimony a sacred character simply because the words are those of victims or of those forgotten by history. To varying degrees depending on the scholar, it is a way of saying that historians are not mere microphone holders or, at the other extreme, militants for the cause of memory. Historians are scholars who construct their objects of research and select their sources in light of the questions that they choose to work on. It is also a means of marking one's distance with respect to the witness, who might be tempted to see the historian as his or her personal scribe.

Lastly, the increasing importance that we grant to images in our societies has led historians to take an interest not just in cinema and television as primary sources for the history of the twentieth century, or as objects of cultural history, but also in order to think about the particular relation that images have with time in general and with historical time in particular. The image creates a present, an impression of the current times and of immediacy, charged with affect and emotion, while history, one recalls, consists of putting time at a distance. Even dated, images convey an impression of proximity that has to be analyzed and critiqued.[3]

P.P.: What is the role of archives?

H.R.: The very emergence of the discipline of the history of the present has paralleled that of an evolution in attitudes and laws concerning access to public archives. The January 3, 1979, law that shortened the normal waiting period for many public records from fifty to thirty years has, for example, been one of the indirect reasons for creating the IHTP. This law erased a highly symbolic stumbling block, that of July 10, 1940,

2. For these distinctions, established by the IHTP, see Danièle Voldman, *La bouche de la vérité?*

3. On this point, see Antoine de Baecque and Christian Delage, *De l'histoire au cinéma*, or Delage and Nicolas Rousselier, eds., *Cinéma, le temps de l'histoire*.

the date of the creation of the Vichy regime, after which almost no public records were accessible. Although liberal in its conception, the law has sometimes been applied in a restrictive manner, notably with the extension to sixty years of waiting periods for any item concerning an individual's private life or facts that could potentially threaten state security or national defense. The notion of "private life" is particularly vague and can cover a tremendous number of documents. In addition to this, there are the even longer delays assigned to certain judiciary or medical archives. This practice has particularly affected documents dating from the Occupation, and some among them even more than others, such as the police archives, less because of the period in question than because of a certain tradition of opacity on the part of the Ministry of the Interior.

Nevertheless, the proliferation of studies on the twentieth century has helped generalize the practice of special dispensations as defined by the new legislation. Although this law is unsatisfactory (because it still operates according to a case-by-case approach), it has enabled researchers to gain access to a great number of documents which, in principle, were unavailable until sixty years or more had expired. In some cases, entire file series have even been provided. Just as significantly, this same accessibility is partly responsible for the development of a historiographical school on Vichy and, more generally, for the advancement of contemporary history. Of course, it remains the case that many documents are still not accessible or require a great deal of time before consultation is approved. However, in October 1997, right at the beginning of the Maurice Papon trial, Prime Minister Lionel Jospin circulated a release requesting that government agencies greatly increase research access to Vichy archives. These administrative bodies, which effectively have the final word controlling access to their holdings, complied to a large extent with Jospin's request. Beyond a doubt, Jospin gave a new impetus that allowed the remaining barriers to be brought down. It was a very positive development to see the government break with French state tradition by taking action on the issue of the accessibility of archives. However, this was also to some extent a public relations gesture, since a great many of these documents had already been familiar to historians for quite some time.

P.P.: Why such sensitivity with respect to the archives? You dedicate an entire chapter to this issue in *Vichy: An Ever-Present Past*.[4] One has

---

4. Conan and Rousso, "The Archives: They Hide Everything, They Tell Us Nothing," *Vichy: An Ever-Present Past*, 46–73. Trans.

the impression that you condemn the amateur research tactics of certain "militants for memory."

H.R.: No, I spoke out against the lies put forth in the name of the duty to remember and against methods that struck me as closer to those of propaganda than those of the quest for truth. But the problem goes deeper. For a couple of years now, the archives have become an issue of public debate. Interest in them continues to grow, fed by an unprecedented agitation on the part of certain medias. This relatively new preoccupation is just one indication of the anxiety-ridden interest in the past. I think it is also a sign of a more or less justified and growing suspicion of the government and others in power. It is part of a larger debate concerning transparency and secrecy in contemporary societies, and it is not by chance that this debate in France is focused exclusively on the question of access to public documents pertaining to the sensitive periods of recent history (Vichy, the Algerian War, etc.). This discussion has brought about undeniably positive changes, such as the thought given to a redefinition of the relations between the governors and the governed. Yet it has also given rise to numerous phantasms on the supposedly perverse nature of power and authority. It is as if the very idea of state secrets or, more prosaically, information that is not immediately released to the public had become unacceptable today. These notions are at the very least debatable. For the sake of brevity, we can mention in the case of the latter, for instance, that it is not the intended function of some information to be released. Or, in other cases, its release could be determined according to a timetable dictated by other factors than the media's constant urgency.

If I were to play on words, I would say that *transparency* is almost synonymous with *invisibility*. In this sense, the ideology of transparency unwittingly promotes a new form of opacity. The surplus of information (including historical information) limits the possibility of putting these facts into perspective and thus hampers knowledge. Moreover, I am not convinced that transparency and democracy always go together. Nor is it absolutely clear that only those in power need fear the sometimes inquisitorial character of this ideology of transparency on all fronts. In the guise of defending democratic liberties, it nonetheless gives more and more power—and a power that encounters ever fewer checks—to certain media. Or, rather, it endows a certain type of journalism with this power, a journalistic approach that is prompt at demanding rigor and transparency from others without practicing it itself. In any case, in my opinion there is no politics of transparency with respect to the government or to public powers in general that is not accompanied by a corresponding obligation of responsibility on the part of the general population, historians and journalists first among them.

P.P.: Is the IHTP born as a result of the 1979 law concerning archives?

H.R.: Yes, to a great extent, but the increased interest in the history of the present had already brought about considerable changes in people's thinking, on the part of archivists and researchers as well as on the part of the political bodies with jurisdiction over these domains. The recent announcement of a bill promising greatly increased archival access is not just a consequence of the Papon trial or of polemical (and at times artificial) debates surrounding Vichy. The proposal is the product of a larger trend, involving more than the history of the tendentious periods.

The IHTP consists of some twenty full-time researchers, some appointed through the CNRS while others have come from outside (including a number of foreign scholars). There are also more than a hundred associates working in secondary and higher education. Its creation is particularly illustrative of the historiographical field's evolution as a whole, which includes an infinitely larger number of specialists, most of whom are teaching in universities. The IHTP was founded in 1978–79 as a result of the reconfiguration of the Committee on the History of World War II (Comité d'Histoire de la Deuxième Guerre Mondiale, or CHDGM). In the 1950s, this group was itself the by-product of several other organizations, including the Commission on the History of the Occupation and the Liberation of France (Commission d'Histoire de l'Occupation et de la Libération de la France), which was created to compile historical documentation on the dark years at the initiative of the provisional government in the fall of 1944. Though financed by the CNRS, the CHDGM answered directly to the prime minister throughout its existence. The idea was to escape being housed under the roof of a single ministry and thereby facilitate access to recent public archives, almost all of which were closed to researchers at that time. In some respects, this situation was rife with ambiguities, for it might lead people to think that the committee was composing an official government history. In truth, these historians, beginning with the director and founder, Henri Michel, were very much part of the intellectual climate reigning in the 1950s and 1960s in which researchers were not really interested in the history of the Vichy regime, even less interested in its anti-Jewish politics, but extremely interested in the history of the Resistance (the deportation of resistants—to the exclusion of racial deportations—and the German crackdown against the Resistance). However, it would be unfair to give credence to the cliché that it took the arrival of foreign scholars like the famous Robert Paxton to generate scholarly interest in these subjects.[5] Paxton and many other foreign historians made great use of the committee's findings, the CHDGM having produced a number of essential books (most of them now forgotten by the public). In the end, it is the committee's lines of questioning and primary interpretations that could be contested, and in fact those who have continued its work have done so rather sharply.

P.P.: The IHTP follows what you called in *The Vichy Syndrome* the stage of the "broken mirror." It comes after Robert Paxton's *Vichy France* (translated into French in 1973), and after the polemics that surrounded the screening of Marcel Ophuls's *The Sorrow and the Pity*. Finally, and most important, it is created at a moment of radical change in perspective with respect to approaches and attitudes toward anti-Semitism and the Holocaust. Is this a coincidence?

H.R.: No, its creation more or less consciously grows out of these trends, though it also goes well beyond them.

On the one hand, having become a full-fledged CNRS research center in 1978–79, which allowed the severance of the umbilical cord tying it to the prime minister, the institution was henceforth able to function like other scholarly organizations. This "normalization" had first been sought by its founder and director, François Bédarida, and was extended by his successor, Robert Frank. The change in status clearly meant that the war could henceforth be considered a research domain like any other, especially given that the new law in principle allowed one to gain access to archival materials from after 1945.

On the other hand, by its very title, the IHTP announced an important change in perspective. Its name is owed in part to a translation of the German term *Zeitgeschichte* (contemporary history), which figures in the heading of an older institution in Munich, the Institute for Contemporary History, one of the leading centers of historiography on Nazism from the very beginnings of the German Federal Republic. It should be noted that for Germans the present begins in 1918 with the Weimar Republic, whereas, in France, the new institute was, by the very conditions of its creation, charged with covering a period going from 1939 to the most recent decades, that is, the end of the 1970s.

This is one of the paradoxes of the creation of this institution. The

5. On Paxton and French historiography, see the recent tribute to the American historian edited by Sara Fishman et al., *France at War: Vichy and the Historians*.

IHTP was originally supposed to continue its predecessor's work on World War II, but what it ended up initiating was a history of the recent past, in particular the years after 1945. Yet, as you will recall, its creation coincides with the beginning of the obsessional phase described in *The Vichy Syndrome*, which sees a continuous and progressive resurgence of reminiscences from this period, right up to its peak with the Papon trial. Consequently, far from abandoning war historiography, the IHTP contributes to its renewal while also establishing a methodology for studying the present period in its ensemble (especially the 1950s, the Algerian War, the history of political economy, etc.). The simultaneity between the reevaluation of the Occupation years and the foundation of an approach for contemporary history belongs once again to a deeper phenomenon that began in the late 1970s and gave those dark years a very different status from that which they had before. Far from being a mere parenthesis in French history, as Paxton had already pointed out, those years became a turning point, a founding moment, the "matrix," as they used to say, of *our* present era, that is, the second half of the twentieth century.

P.P.: However, to quote Jan Patocka, aren't the two world wars of our tragic century intimately linked?

H.R.: Seeing World War II as the "matrix" of the present era is probably a historical paradigm whose time has passed. The fall of the Berlin Wall suggests another periodization for this century. This event unexpectedly brings to a close a sequence that began with the Russian revolution of 1917 and in a certain way relativizes the year 1945, which until now seemed the pivotal date for this century, particularly because of the polarization that was born at that moment and that was expected to last. Historians today are reevaluating both the weight of World War I (which some see as the true "matrix" of the century) and its unequaled violence.

However debatable or amendable that may be, the paradigm of World War II as foundational had a very important impact not just on twentieth-century historical research but also on the status of contemporary history. In fact, it is in 1982–83 that the curriculum in history at the level of secondary education first offered consequential chapters on World War II and the present era, whose departure point at that time was 1939 and not 1945 (which is a very different thing). This reform has since been reexamined and will undergo further adjustments, but its arrival marked a clean break with the model that was introduced in the 1950s by Fernand Braudel and dealt with the post-1945 period—after an elliptic overview of the years from 1939 to 1945—through its "great civilizations" format, mixing politics, geography, and history.

A new methodology for studying contemporary history that takes shape in part through the work done on World War II and the tragic sequence stretching from 1930 to 1950, this phenomenon is not limited to France. It also constitutes a key element of German postwar historiography and can be just as easily noted in Belgium and the Netherlands, two other countries where the Nazi occupation left lasting after-effects. It is perceptible in Italy, which has the burden of its fascist past, as well as in Spain, where the memories of Franco's reign linger still. Signs of it have even begun to crop up in Switzerland, where a reassessment of its activities between 1939 and 1945 is now under way. Though the chronology varies with the particular circumstances of each country, these are cases in which the history of this critical sequence has laid the seeds for and in return been nourished by the present era's interest in the recent past and its growing past. From its very inception, the new history of the present has been a "writing of disasters," which compounds the difficulties we mentioned earlier.

P.P.: Is this persistent presence of the past in current cultural and collective representations specific to the history of the present and to the period spanning from the late 1970s to the early 1980s? Or can one find other examples in history of persistent reworkings where nineteenth-century historians or others prominent in the 1930s were forced to analyze a similar syndrome?

H.R.: The phenomenon is certainly not new, and it is by definition an issue for all contemporary histories. I spoke earlier of the impact of the French Revolution on the political, cultural, and historiographical evolution of the nineteenth century. One could add the Dreyfus affair and World War I, which deeply marked the generations that lived through them and gave rise to ceaseless political and historiographical debates. Almost from its beginning and especially since the end of Stalinism, the history of communism constitutes an entity of the same order. However, the Vichy syndrome, this obsessive interest in the dark years, adds a unique trait since, as the French variation of what was an international phenomenon (at least for the countries that experienced the last world war), it now gives considerable weight to the memory of the Holocaust. Lastly, it bears repeating that the posterity of this event is unique in history.

P.P.: Where do historians fit into this kind of phenomena? Are they caught up in the political and cultural changes of their time, whether they like it or not?

H.R.: Yes. Without really being conscious of it, they get caught up in them or, as often as not, they follow them or, more rarely, they anticipate them. This is one of the most important features of the history of the present. The passion it elicits from the public is in part an outgrowth of the age of memory, with all the ambiguities and conflicts between history and memory that we mentioned earlier. We could also extend our questioning to the uses of history that the valorization of memory has brought about or to the consequences for the field of historiography itself.

During the "Thirty Glorious Years" (France's great period of growth spanning from 1945 to 1975), while the social imaginary still offered many different visions of an undecided future and the idea of a civilization of progress regained currency, "prospective" thinking occupied a big place in intellectual reflection. During this period of profound transformation, we turned to social scientists to create models of development and growth, elaborate forecasting tools in statistics and public finance, or to propose interpretative approaches for understanding the new social subgroups (consumers, for instance). Sociologists and economists, for example, answered the needs of the public more readily than other disciplines and thus were called upon to advise the authorities. They furnished concrete, more or less reliable expertise, while they stoked the imagination of the decision makers and their credo of a possible scientific grasp on the present and the future.

Starting with the 1970s, it was now the historians who were in demand, especially those in the area of the history of the present. Solicited by the government, or by society at large in the public and private sectors, historians were called upon to write the history of organizations, groups, or communities, participate in a growing number of ministerial committees on history treating particular historical moments or questions, or provide their expertise in ever broader contexts—even up to the borderline case of expert witnesses in the Touvier and Papon trials. For more than twenty years now, the figure of the historian has assumed an important place within the closed circle of experts who are interviewed on television and more or less successfully provide commentary on the troubling questions that pop up on a daily basis ever since the past became front page news.

P.P.: Returning to his theme of a crisis in history, Gérard Noiriel recently asked in *Le Monde de l'éducation*, "Will the new generation [of historians] that are picking up the reins of responsibility today know how to (or want to) invent the new public spaces for discussion and collective reflection that are currently lacking—by making use, for instance, of the innovations that technology has made available to them? Will they know how to open these debates so that the questions . . . concerning new directions in research, the democratization of the internal functioning of the discipline and of external recruitment, relations with the publishing milieu, journalists and the world of 'amateur' historians, etc., can be debated by all the historians who wish to do so?" Do you also feel that the future of historical research depends on the answer to these questions?

H.R.: I think it is important to distinguish between "corporatist" issues (recruiting, the internal functioning of the discipline, etc.), which hardly have any specificity of note with respect to neighboring disciplines, and the situation of history in today's public debates, which is a unique occurrence of obvious significance for our society. I do not subscribe to the notion that there is a "crisis" in historiography. Rather than a general crisis in the discipline, it seems to me to be much more a question of the relative decline, perhaps to be regretted, of a certain model of social history. I agree even less with the idea that history might have something to lose in the dialogue that it has recently reestablished with philosophy, a dialogue which Noiriel seems to see as a cause for concern. On the other hand, I agree with him that we need to find spaces not so much for debate among historians (who have ample opportunity to do so on their own) but for historians to intervene in the public sphere without being hampered by the media's discourse and expectations. In fact, scholars and researchers have always had to confront this problem. The only thing that changes is the fact that it is not always the same disciplines that are in demand. The dilemma itself does not change in nature. There are two paths open to scholars. On the one hand, they can maintain absolute control over their scientific discourse, but at the cost of retreating into an ivory tower. Or they can open up to the outside world and respond to societal demands. In so doing, however, they will forfeit control over discourse and have to resign themselves to the unreliability of the media through which they would communicate. Where the history of the present is concerned, the first approach strikes me as misguided and unacceptable. Therefore, entering the sphere of public debate necessarily means accepting the vulgarization of scientific discourse, accepting the fact that it cannot be entirely controlled—and its effects even less. It means accepting that one may be called upon to intercede. For the moment, for better or for worse, the media are where public debate takes place. The people who exert real control over these arenas perhaps also bear responsibility for this.

P.P.: One cannot simply ignore the societal demands?

H.R.: In university circles, societal demands are not always looked upon very favorably. Scholars are suspicious that such demands could constitute an attempt to influence the intellectual problems being treated, indirectly orient research through financial support, or introduce stakes of another nature in the research sector, be they political, media-related, or commercial. In essence, the societal demands are seen as compromising the academic enterprise, which is, as we all know, free from all considerations outside of the quest for knowledge.

Be they implicit or explicit, these critiques merit consideration. First, the societal demands constitute a complex and slippery reality, inscribed in the "age of memory" that we discussed at the outset. It is not just the government or authorities that are making these demands—far from it. Thus, while it is perhaps possible to ignore an official request or to refuse to sit on legal expert committees, it is more tenuous morally to turn one's nose up at a request originating in civil society. This is especially true when the request carries a strong emotional charge, for example, in the instance of associations for deportees or veterans of the French Resistance or any other category of war victims. (I simply mention here those with which I am the most familiar.) If such a refusal does arise—and it happens fairly often now, so great has the demand become—historians are accused of arrogance or insensitivity, something which I have experienced myself, even though the institute responds as best it can to the numerous requests it receives.

Another element to remember is that societal demands are not at all a new development in historiography. Those who critique historians who have incorporated these demands into their research forget that in the past historians were praised for their heightened civic or revolutionary sense when they identified themselves as intellectuals working for the greater good of the workers' party. (Although they are now in the minority, these reflexes have not completely disappeared.) This dilemma poses the essential question of the role of the intellectual, an inexhaustible subject of contention. However, at the risk of seeming behind the times, and speaking solely for myself, I do not subscribe to the sacrosanct French model which valorizes intellectuals as those who speak up about things that are none of their business. More modestly, I prefer to talk about what I know or believe I know. Otherwise, I think you are misleading people. To act in this manner is to lead others to believe that the specialized *knowledge* of a university scholar in a specific domain gives additional legitimacy to what is only an *opinion* in other domains, no more noteworthy than that of any other citizen, especially when it is a question of a political or ideological position that has nothing to do with scientific method.

Lastly, while I subscribe wholeheartedly to the idea of science's necessary autonomy, I do not want to lose sight of the fact that science is affected by the many social issues of a given moment and that a scientific problem, especially in the area of the human and social sciences, does not sprout up spontaneously in the minds of researchers who somehow are supposed to exist outside of time.

P.P.: How should a historian respond to these demands?

H.R.: There lies the question. In research, the choice of one topic or another must be as much as possible the initiative of the scholar or research milieu. But this also implies that one needs to be attentive to the social stakes of knowledge and to expectations, in order to foresee them rather than be dependent upon them. Sometimes this is not the case, however—for instance, a book can be commissioned by a publisher who has intellectual concerns (such a thing exists as well), or a question can surface in current events that has not previously been addressed by scholars. If the scholar accepts the project, it is imperative that he or she open a dialogue or negotiate the power relations brought into play by the source of the request. The scholar must then *translate* the demand into the means and terms that are proper to his or her own activity. This is an indispensable condition for exercising the necessary control over one's research, in particular with respect to organizing one's time and preserving one's freedom of investigation. The latter must be at least equal to what it would be if one were engaged in an investigation with no preestablished targets. I am very much aware of the fact that one of the real problems facing researchers today stems from the media's continual urgency, which can severely jeopardize the reliability of the expertise given and the liberty of the scholar, which in turn inevitably leads to errors of judgment or even questionable behavior and decisions.

Another important issue lies in the major risk of an instrumentalization of expertise, that is, where it is not a historian's knowledge or techniques that are being sought out but his or her institutional position. This is one of the essential problems facing historians when polemical debates concerning one episode or another of recent history break out onto the public stage, regardless of their intellectual approach.

Finally, responding to a request coming from the social sector means that one is not going to simply offer up one's findings or provide unequivocal answers to often extremely difficult questions. Rather, it means that one must present the "truth" uncovered by one's research regardless of the content of that truth, even if it turns out to go against those who commissioned the work in the first place. It is their problem if the truth does not conform to the results they were counting on, though this, of course, does not exempt the historian from any responsibility. While this truth must be founded on scientific evidence, it must also be accompanied, as much as possible, by an explanation of the means used to establish this truth. This explanation should thus underline the limits of the answer furnished and the uncertainty inherent to the discipline itself. Responding to a request from the social sector for a historical investigation should always be, in the long run and ideally, an attempt to give an account of the complexity and incompleteness of any analysis of the past. One must not allow oneself in these circumstances to play the role of thaumaturgic historians capable of curing crises of identity or legitimacy, be they individual, social, or national.

Chapter 3
What Court of Judgment for History?

Philippe Petit: "History never confesses," Maurice Merleau-Ponty used to say. But ever since the tragedy of World War II, the judicial system has become the principal apparatus through which absolute evil and other things negative are represented. We began by putting men on trial as war criminals, then moved on to judging (indirectly) a government and an ideology. In the context of the Eichmann trial in 1961, Hannah Arendt remarked, "If the defendant is taken as a symbol and the trial is a pretext to bring up matters which are apparently more interesting than the guilt or innocence of one person, then consistency demands that we bow to the assertion made by Eichmann and his lawyer: that he was brought to book because a scapegoat was needed, not only for the German Federal Republic, but also for the events as a whole and for what made them possible — that is, for anti-Semitism and totalitarian government as well as for the human race and original sin" (Arendt 286). Aren't we confronted today more than ever with this judicial logic in which it is not simply individuals who are being tried but also history as a whole?

Henry Rousso: Yes, for several years now, it has seemed hard to get away from judicial readings of history. The past is a source of issues that find their expression in real and symbolic courtrooms. But this process of putting history on trial — and this is especially true of the literal courtroom instances — primarily concerns the aftermaths of the most tragic and unbearable episodes of this century: Nazism, World War II, and, since the fall of the Berlin Wall, communism.

This tendency is evident in the belated trials for war crimes and crimes against humanity in France, Germany, Israel, and recently even in Italy. It is also apparent in the international legal and political actions taken against countries in order to demand reparations (as in the cases of Japan and Switzerland for their conduct during the last world war).

The same holds true for the suits filed against negationists. Of course, these are just a few examples, each very different in nature and magnitude. But they do have a common trait: In each instance, the domains of historian and judge, of knowledge and norms—these latter being designed in principle for present and future actions and not for the past—not only cross paths but on occasion get crossed up.

The desire to put the past on trial is apparent also in the practice of writers, journalists, and historians who, consciously or not, see themselves as the bearers of the "vengeance of the nations," to quote Chateaubriand's famous phrase.[1] Let it be noted in passing that the "prosecutor-historian" is much more readily stigmatized than the "advocate-historian," even though the problem is the same: Be it as judge, prosecutor, or advocate, historians are no longer in their proper element once they don courtroom robes. And I do not think that it is merely a problem of intellectual, commercial, and media excesses that could be curbed through a call to order or a return to sound historical methodologies. Moreover, the same people who publicly take their colleagues to task on one day succumb the following day to the intoxication of the media spotlight or judicial posturing. It all depends on the context and the facts being discussed. Despite appearances to the contrary, the cases related to episodes in recent history that have stirred up public opinion for a little while now are not all alike. Consequently, we find the same protagonists playing very different roles from one case to the next. People are sometimes quite astonished by this, given the tendency to think of historians as a homogeneous group dispensing indisputable truths.

We must, of course, denounce the actions of those who go too far, provided that we do not hide behind the mask of ethics in order to promote trivial ideological positions. But I am convinced that this phenomenon goes beyond the scope of the media or intellectual microcosms. To some extent, it is a product of public expectations, expectations which are more or less artificially kept alive. Controversial works, often skillfully marketed, enjoy a very large audience. The public fol-

---

1. In his memoirs, Chateaubriand looks back over Napoleon's career and, as a monarchist, is particularly bitter over the emperor's assassination of the duke of Enghien. To this effect, Chateaubriand cites one of his own articles, which appeared in the *Mercure* in 1807 at the height of the First Empire: "When all tremble before the tyrant, and it is as dangerous to enjoy his favor as it is to earn his disapproval, the historian comes to the fore, entrusted with the vengeance of the nations" (Chateaubriand 1:570; my translation). Trans.

lows historical polemics with avid, even frenzied interest—a fact not lost on the media. Trials like that of Maurice Papon also generate tremendous public interest (at least initially). Be they real or virtual, these trials are in fact stagings of the past. It is hardly surprising that the society of the spectacle is so intrigued by the spectacle of history.[2]

P.P.: Nonetheless, these trials mark a serious examination of the past.

H.R.: They correspond to an unprecedented translation of the troubled questions we are now asking about the past, present, and future. This judicialization of the past very much belongs to the "age of memory." In fact, it is one of its founding elements, contributing to putting the past into the present. It does not target abstract historical entities. Rather, it takes aim at individuals (living or dead) and nations which are being asked, rightly or wrongly, to account for themselves. Consistent with this trend, the judges—some authorized, others self-appointed— justify their actions as being in the name of memory and, generally speaking, in the name of victims to whom justice was not done in their day. In this instance, it is no longer a question of the traditional "history as the world's court of judgment," which promises a form of closure for the event and shows that posterity has taken its distance with respect to the past. What we have here are "temporal tribunals," that is, courts catering to the preoccupations of a particular period and whose primary characteristic is, on the contrary, to keep this past *open*, insofar as the courts are still sitting in "deliberation," in a recurrent or permanent manner. These real and virtual courts operate under the illusion that the verdict delivered will take the place of "history as the world's court of judgment." In the end, however, the trials have a provisional, unfinished feel to them, as if we were merely waiting for the dossier to be opened again and for polemics to flare up anew. Furthermore, since imprescriptibility has become one of the forms of our relation to the past and the memory of the Holocaust serves as the standard by which all historical approaches are measured, people today expect to see the guilty parties clearly designated for each of the century's tragedies that we have not been able to assimilate. When we speak of guilt, the words *court* and *trial* are soon to follow.

P.P.: Isn't this what happened with *The Black Book of Communism*?

H.R.: Since justice by legal avenues had not really been sought in this

2. "La société du spectacle" was a trademark phrase of the late Guy Debord, a polemical French social critic who was a leader of the Situationists in the late 1960s. He argued that representations have displaced lived experience to such an extent that social behavior is almost entirely mediated by images and other symbolic forms. Trans.

instance, historians could think themselves authorized to rectify this oversight—which is in fact what happened with this work. *The Black Book of Communism*, whose considerable success extended throughout France, Italy, Germany, Central Europe, the former Soviet bloc's western regions, and Russia, marks the first attempt to analyze the "crimes of communism" and synthesize them on a global scale, spanning the entirety of this century. It covers the Soviet regime, the people's democracies of Eastern Europe, the Comintern's activities, communist China, as well as North Korea, Vietnam, Cambodia, Laos, the Cuban example, a few Latin American countries, and even communism in Africa and Afghanistan. The project encompasses a geopolitical and historical field that is immense and heterogeneous. Some chapters, like those on the USSR and Eastern Europe, use original research and reflect the significant progress made by recent historiography. Some others are based on secondhand documentation, while others are written with a political edge. As a result, the quality varies widely from chapter to chapter. What most struck public opinion in this book, however, was the number put forth, in a most unscientific manner, of the overall tally of communism's casualties: For all countries and categories combined, an estimated 85 million had been killed. This number was quickly transformed into a rallying cry in European political debates.

This book's shortcomings are due essentially to the publisher and one of the project's directors, Stéphane Courtois. In spite of opposition from coauthors Nicolas Werth (responsible for the largest section, that on the USSR) and Jean-Louis Margolin (who wrote the chapters on Asia), Courtois and the publisher transformed what was initially a legitimate scientific undertaking into a vast ideological and commercial operation intended to deal a "decisive blow" to communism, already agonizing on its deathbed (at least in the West). This editorial tactic undeniably succeeded in procuring immense commercial success, with nearly 500,000 copies sold in Europe. But it cast a cloud of doubt over the scientific character of the completed work, debatable on many a point. Originally, François Furet was slated to write the introduction, but after the great historian's death Courtois took on the task.[3] The principal cause of the

3. Furet challenged popular Marxist interpretations of the French Revolution with a centrist stance that identified elements of a democratic heritage issuing from 1789. Furet's methodology eschewed factual minutiae in favor of philosophical and political analysis. He also specialized in the history of communist regimes. Having resigned from the Party after the Soviet invasion of Hungary in 1956, he wrote as one of his last major works *The Passing of an Illusion*. Trans.

polemics provoked by the book, Courtois's introduction tries to demonstrate, with a great deal of verbal gymnastics, not only that the communist system was criminal in its very essence but also that, according to the definitions established in 1945, its actions could be categorized as "crimes against humanity." Courtois implied that the book and the debates it raised would in one way or another fulfill the role of a sort of "Nuremberg on communism," an idea which he has frequently discussed in the media as well. In other words, in the absence of "purge" trials, historians should take on the role of judges and act as spokespersons for the victims. Personally, I feel that such an exercise is as dangerous as it is doomed. Whereas historians of Nazism have been trying ever since the Nuremberg trials to break out of juridical models of interpretation in order to promote more historical readings, we now find that same grid recklessly applied to a phenomenon of an entirely different nature, in another context altogether, for countries that have nothing to do with each other and even less to do with Germany.

It is not the comparison of communism to Nazism that strikes me as illegitimate, particularly given that this was first presented a long time ago, beginning with Hannah Arendt, whom you quoted earlier. Rather, it is the metaphorical usage of the courtroom setting and the stance adopted by some historians that strike me as rife with ambiguities. Moreover, this stance ultimately led historians away from the original terms of their research. Not only does Courtois's introduction fail to offer any comparisons between the countries studied—which, as one can see from the table of contents, was the initial project—but the proposed problematic most closely resembles a sort of juridical framing of the question. The concept has become an indictment, insofar as "crimes against humanity" is a legal category. Historical inquiry is turned into a criminal investigation, and the intellectual or moral assessments that all historians are free to formulate become more like "verdicts," without any possibility of appeal for those found guilty.

Irrespective of its actual qualities, presented in this manner, *The Black Book of Communism* caters to the expectations of our time. One has the impression that some history buffs can only grasp history via simple binary categories: victims and executioners, the innocent and the guilty, good and evil. Be that as it may, I would like to point out an interesting paradox: As a result of a few polemical pages without any scientific significance and a considerable amount of advertising fanfare, *The Black Book of Communism* provided a convenient way out for diehard communists whose faith could have been deeply shaken—and with good reason—by some of this work's conclusions. This is particularly the case in France, where communism's political and intellectual legacy is still very much alive.

In the final analysis, a judicial history is a history where rhetoric gets the upper hand on argumentation, with the accusers and the accused being thrown into the same boat willy-nilly.

P.P.: Let's move on to recent events that involved you directly, namely, your refusal to testify in the Papon trial and your participation in a roundtable discussion with two prestigious figures from the French Resistance, Lucie and Raymond Aubrac. We will discuss these one at a time, but I wonder if they do not have some points in common? In both cases, historians were asked to shed light on what one tactfully calls "murky waters." Since when are historians detectives ferreting out the truth?

H.R.: Yes, indeed. Historians conduct inquiries and seek the truth just like the detectives you mention. In my opinion, the comparison stops there. It could just as easily be applied to a particular type of journalism commonly referred to as "investigative." I mentioned earlier a few instances in which historical work has not been preempted by court cases. This applies to the majority of the countries that recently experienced the fall of communism. The problem lies once again in the juridical stance that certain scholars adopt. When historians work on events or public figures that come under legal investigation for a second or third time—as was the case with Klaus Barbie (a Nazi criminal), Paul Touvier (a member of the French *milice*), and Maurice Papon (a Vichy civil servant)—the court can call on these scholars for their expertise. Though different from the dilemmas posed by self-appointed judges, this situation is just as problematic. In this latter instance, the primary risk comes from the instrumentalization of historians. The court summons them in the service of ends that are clearly legitimate (the judgment of criminals), but, in my opinion, these ends have little to do with scientific method, which seeks to understand rather than to judge and even less to absolve or condemn. The tendency to call on professional historians to legitimize discourses of another order is not limited to the courts that recently sat in judgment on "crimes against humanity" cases in France and elsewhere. This is the only point in common that I see between the Papon trial and what has been called the "Aubrac affair."

The Papon trial was a real trial of considerable magnitude. It concerned a former Vichy civil servant who found himself asked to shoulder the burden of the criminal acts of an entire regime, perhaps even of an entire era.

The stakes of this event were of proportions completely different from those of the polemic that erupted over the history of the Aubrac couple. This latter situation is quite typical of how the French quarrel endlessly over their past, especially when memories of the German Occupation are at issue.

In May 1997, the French daily newspaper *Libération* organized a roundtable involving two popular figures from the French Resistance, Lucie and Raymond Aubrac, as well as other equally prestigious Resistance veterans, including Daniel Cordier, former secretary to Jean Moulin (head of the unified French interior Resistance who died under torture in 1943). Also invited to participate were a number of historians specializing in this period, myself among them. The proceedings from this session were published in their entirety on July 9, 1997, as a special supplement to *Libération*. The objective was to examine the accusations leveled at the Aubracs by a journalist who claimed, without any real justification, that they had betrayed their comrades-in-arms during the Occupation.

I will come back to this complex affair later. For the moment, however, it should suffice to keep in mind that this confrontation between historians and agents of history raised a number of issues concerning the relation between scholarly history and the memory of witnesses, the different status that truth holds for different people, and the difficulty of writing a critical history without making concessions when one is in the presence of figures who in the eyes of the public are emblematic of true heroism (e.g., Lucie and Raymond Aubrac). The questions that were put to the Aubracs, the historians' concern in wanting to establish as precisely as possible the materiality of the facts, and the outrage that these veterans of the Resistance expressed in the face of what they considered to be a sort of tribunal constituted the ingredients of a polemic whose interest lies once again in the attitude of the historians (i.e., in the role they play, that they want to play, or that people want them to play).

A number of people have seen parallels between the Papon trial and the Aubrac affair, most notably because of the role played by historians in both instances. A journalist from *Le Monde* even asked me why I had refused to testify in the Papon trial "when in fact" I had participated a few months earlier in the Aubrac roundtable organized by *Libéra-*

tion.[4] The insinuation was obvious: Since I had participated in a sort of mock trial that called into question two great figures of the French Resistance, why refuse to participate in a real trial that was going to call into question a former Vichy civil servant? This rather insidious conflation of the two contexts is in fact a good illustration of the role that some people expect historians to embrace: Historians should act not in the service of the truth but rather to serve "the good cause" — in this case, defending the Resistance and condemning Vichy. With respect to the question of this amalgam of two distinct issues, my answer includes several elements. I pointed out that the *Libération* roundtable was at Raymond Aubrac's request and that he personally suggested the historians ultimately in attendance. In addition, this roundtable panel did not propose any verdict. It was the occasion for a free exchange between consenting parties, courteous throughout even if at times the going got a bit rough. One must grant that there are very few tribunals in which it is the defendant who convenes the court, decides upon its composition, establishes the procedure to be followed, and allows the eventual publication of the trial transcript without, to top it off, ever having a decision handed down.

That said, it is clear that this roundtable bothered and even shocked portions of the general public and historical circles. This type of confrontation — especially when it takes place in a leading newspaper — poses numerous problems and merits further reflection. I am not claiming to hold the secret to the proper ethical stance for historians to adopt. But now that the polemic has died down, we can try to understand its mechanisms and see what it tells us about the current situation of historians of the present. One has to go back to the nineteenth century to find a time when historians have had such a considerable role in public debates as agents (and not just as mere observers). All of those involved react according to their own conscience and abilities, their own ideological choices and limits. We need to rid ourselves of the notion that there is a historians' "guild." Above all else, ethics are a personal matter, even if, as a university scholar, I try to respect the rules of my craft and a certain deontology. All the same, this still leaves us a margin for personal initiative and thus for eventual errors, especially when we are faced with unprecedented situations like those that we see today. But since all of us are swept up in the court metaphor, we must at least assess

4. Nicolas Weill, "Le dilemme des historiens cités à comparaître."

situations case by case, investigate before passing judgment, absolve or condemn only when fully informed about the matter at hand, and not react on the basis of ideological or moral biases.

P.P.: From the very outset of the Papon trial, discordant voices were heard. In *Le Débat*, Paul Thibaud called it anachronistic. In *Le Monde*, Alain Finkielkraut also expressed misgivings: "I have a hard time seeing what judicial truth can come of a debate in which the defendant will be in a certain sense his only contemporary." After sitting through the first three months of the hearings, Éric Conan entitled a long article in *L'Express* "The Papon Trial: Time to Be Done with It!"[5] Are you disappointed as well?

H.R.: Some time back, I was one of the first to express reservations—one might even say serious doubts—about this type of trial, especially in the book written with Éric Conan. That said, the press's frequent use of the word notwithstanding, the term *disappointment* is itself problematic. It means that the expectations regarding such a trial far exceed the desire that justice be done in the best manner possible. The use of this term ties in explicitly with seeing it as a spectacle, as if trials of this sort were supposed to feed our imagination. A trial in principle is not a movie or play able to satisfy or disappoint—even if it is based on a form of theatricalization. Nor is it a history lesson bearing ideological significations. This, at least, is the conclusion I have come to, having observed since 1987 the French trials for crimes against humanity.

Under normal circumstances, a criminal trial can turn out to be precedent-setting by the contribution it makes to a politics of the punishment and prevention of crime. It lays down very distinctly—or contributes to the reestablishment of—the boundaries between good and evil, the tolerable and the intolerable, the permissible and the punishable. We see this today in the judicial system's efforts to clarify demarcations that have become blurred, be it in the suppression of finance scandals in politics or, in a completely different vein, crimes of pedophilia.

In historic trials like those of Klaus Barbie, Paul Touvier, and Maurice Papon, we are grappling with another register. Beyond the judgment of particular individuals, the declared goal is to illuminate an entire era and its politics. These trials are not precedent setting in the sense of seeking to prevent similar crimes from occurring. Rather, they are a form of belated reparation. Doubtlessly warranted from the point of view of

5. Thibaud, "Un temps de mémoire?"; Finkielkraut, "Papon: trop tard"; and Conan, "Le procès Papon: il faut en finir!"

the victims, this reparation is supposed to make up for what was poorly done during the "purge" and postwar trials—or, to be more precise, what is, a half century after the fact, construed as botched by other generations possessing different mind-sets. These trials are imagined as a catharsis on a national scale, a means of proclaiming to the world that France is capable of facing up to its past. In some respects, they are also a by-product of the growing judicialization of our societies, a tendency whereby the justice system is increasingly called upon to resolve problems that previously were settled or regulated by other means, in other places.

P.P.: Nevertheless, didn't these trials succeed in raising a few pressing issues?

H.R.: I would argue that they raised many more problems than they resolved, because they could not avoid having to situate themselves with respect to three distinct domains. First, there is the justice system itself. To the exclusion of all other considerations and acts (at least, as long as due process is respected), it examines specific crimes defined by specific texts and procedures and committed by specific individuals. Second, there is national memory, understood here as a particular form of commemoration, a ritualized interpretation of the past that is dependent upon the expectations of the present and whose objective is to inscribe this past in collective consciousness, with the full force of the law and the symbolism of the legal apparatus. Lastly, there is history, that is to say, a detached analysis of that same past which seeks to restore the truth of an era in its context, complexity, and ambiguities. The justice system asks whether an individual is guilty or innocent; national memory is the by-product of a tension existing between remembrances that are memorable and "commemorable" and oversights that enable the survival of the community and its projection into the future; history is an undertaking of knowledge and elucidation. Even if all three of these domains address the question of truth, this multiplicity of concerns poses serious difficulties. These domains can be superimposed, as has happened in the trials for crimes against humanity. However, this has burdened the trials from the very outset with an unbearable load: Not all of these trials could measure up equally to the task of treating the lofty issues at stake in justice, memory, and history. Justice was rendered in extraordinary circumstances, ones hardly common in a normal trial and sometimes not really acceptable with respect to the law. At the same time, even among the most committed partisans of these trials, it quickly becomes apparent that a great many other places and means exist for celebrating memory or writing history. To my mind, disappointment was thus built into the project of the Papon trial from the beginning, irrespective of its own vicissitudes. These latter incidents only magnified our impression of witnessing a shipwreck.

P.P.: Why did you refuse to testify at the Papon trial?

H.R.: It was a matter of principle. I explained my position at the beginning of the trial in a letter written to the chief justice of the Court of Assizes, a letter which was read during the hearing.[6] I am not claiming that my stance is the only ethical approach for historians, nor am I reproaching in any way colleagues who agreed to take the stand. Four scholars from the research group that I direct at the IHTP were asked to testify in Bordeaux. Two of them informally declined the invitation while another, Marc-Olivier Baruch, accepted and appeared on the stand along with other historians with whom I have been working since the beginning of my career. For my part, I made public my refusal to appear. All of these choices are valid and, despite the insinuations of a few journalists hoping for a story, they do not at all mean that discord reigns henceforth among historians. Moreover, even if this were the case, what conclusions should one draw? That historians must speak as one, united in a single voice?

I refused to testify for several reasons. I had already been asked to testify in 1994 by plaintiffs in the Paul Touvier trial. Unlike four of my colleagues, I declined, explaining that, on the one hand, I wanted to preserve my freedom of speech and analysis — which in principle is impossible once one is summoned to the stand — and, on the other hand, the trial struck me as biased. As events soon showed, the necessity of respecting legal procedures and the indictments as defined by law and jurisprudence did in fact lead people to tinker with the facts: for example, the claim that Touvier's execution of seven Jewish hostages from Rillieux on June 29, 1944, the only crime for which he had been charged and convicted, was done as an accomplice of the Third Reich. This is inaccurate, since Touvier's actions were in the service of the French *milice*, eager at that moment to avenge Philippe Henriot, Vichy's minister of information and propaganda, who was executed by members of the Resistance. In other words, Touvier's act was intended to settle internal scores and thus was neither directly related to the "Final Solution" nor ordered by the occupying powers. I did not want to betray what I believed to be the historical truth (a truth grounded in existing sources).

6. See appendix for Rousso's letter to the Bordeaux chief justice.

Furthermore, I did not want to participate in the paradox of this trial: Intended as an occasion to show the magnitude of personal initiative in the murderous anti-Semitism practiced by Vichy and certain other parts of the French population, it ended up producing a conviction for complicity with the Nazis. This verdict is not only false historically speaking. It is also not particularly significant with respect to memory. Everyone executed legally by firing squad after 1944—nearly 1,500 people—was put to death for being "in collusion with the enemy," that is, for collaboration or complicity with the Nazis. From this point of view, the Touvier trial was hardly novel. In truth, it was nothing but a belated avatar of the postwar purge and not at all the significant step forward for justice and memory that many had anticipated.

P.P.: In the 1997 case of Maurice Papon, however, the situation was different.

H.R.: Yes, but the presence of historians on the stand struck me as just as problematic. First of all, I had been named by the defense without any prior notification.' In fact, I learned about it in the press before I had received the official summons. The fact that I was called by the defense (as were other historians with whom I work closely) did not pose a greater or lesser problem for me than if it had been the prosecutor or plaintiffs who sought my participation. By the same token, however, it seemed obvious that the recourse to certain historians, mediatized as it was, arose less from pedagogical concerns than from a desire on all sides to instrumentalize knowledge by giving a sort of juridical endorsement to interpretations that were in fact already widely accepted and essentially irrefutable. In a certain sense, these interpretations could even be said to have oriented the entire preliminary inquest. One can hardly fathom otherwise why the prosecution and plaintiffs would ask historians to state evident truths such as the following: "Yes, Vichy and the French administration collaborated with the occupying forces," or "Yes, the government did in fact promulgate anti-Semitic legislation." The massive presence of historians, a presence that was calculated as part of the legal strategies, meant that the court passed off on them some of the work of establishing general background and context, as if the truth had more weight in the mouths of historians than in those of lawyers and magistrates. This was all the more curious given that, with the notable exception of some of the defendant's remarks, the statements tended to offer the same information.

This is one of the points that seems the most problematic to me. What does it mean to give under oath an account of a historical context, not as an expert but as a witness (in the strict sense of the term), when in fact the historian cannot answer the fundamental question: Is the individual guilty or innocent? Historians can describe a given context only in response to a specific line of questioning. From the moment that the question consists of determining the guilt of an individual, all argumentation, consciously or unconsciously, hinges on what would allow us to come up with an answer, in one direction or the other. The question of knowing whether the general secretary of a regional prefecture was an important, decision-making figure during the Occupation seems to me, speaking as a historian, secondary to a much broader question, which is to learn how such an administration functioned as a whole. The fact that a particular individual was head of a particular department certainly has its importance, but it cannot constitute the ultimate objective of a research project or inquiry. If the contrary were true, one would risk stripping historical work of all significance and locking it into a form of erudition that is as gratuitous as it is vain. It goes without saying that this is not the court's point of view, which is of course perfectly understandable.

I would like to mention a final objection, one that strikes me as central to this debate. In my opinion, the historians summoned to appear were not really called on for the information they could provide in expert testimony. To the best of my knowledge, expert witnesses called by the court fall into one of two categories. In the first instance, an expert can be asked to provide an account of general phenomena formally proven by the laws of science and assumed to be reproducible on any occasion. This is true, for example, in the fields of ballistics and genetics. This type of expert can help the court even when the specialist knows nothing about the particulars of the case being tried. The second variety of expert has direct knowledge of the dossier or the defendant, as in the instance of psychiatric experts who can provide a diagnosis concerning the defendant. In the Papon trial, however, the historians in attendance belonged to neither the first nor the second category; there were no universal laws at issue, and the historians could not claim specific knowledge of the dossier (for reasons we will explain below).

P.P.: But that is not why they were there. Robert Paxton focused primarily on the spirit of the period, the context of Vichy.

H.R.: Talking about the context in this particular setting presupposed in all good faith that what was true of the general case (the history of the government's collaboration and the national revolution, the functioning of the administration as a whole, etc.) was necessarily true — or extremely probable—in the specific instance of the general secretary of the Gironde Prefecture. Even if almost all of the historians avoided speaking specifically about Maurice Papon, their presence on the stand was intended in the eyes of the court to operate the translation from the global context to that of Bordeaux. In carrying out such a translation, one forgets that the restored context is itself the fruit of a *generalization* derived from specific situations (monographic studies, for example). It cannot in any way furnish the same order of certainty as that provided by the laws of ballistics or genetics. Such expectations grant historians investigative capabilities and scientific means that they do not possess, limitations which they readily acknowledge in the normal practice of their craft. One of the greatest risks facing historical approaches is to succumb to the "metonymic temptation," that is, to take the part for the whole and vice versa, and to believe that, all other things beings equal, what is true in one particular situation is necessarily true in another. The craft of historian consists precisely in verifying the extent to which the other things are in fact equal and in determining the nature of the discrepancy that can exist between the case studied and the ideal type (itself but a metaphorical construction of several particular cases).

In the Papon trial, however, it was simply not possible to carry out this essential phase. Legal experts had access to the dossier or could at least analyze the case. The historians, though—with the sole exception of Michel Bergès, whose testimony stirred up so much commotion—had no access whatsoever to the documents: It is forbidden by the penal code. The historians were therefore not allowed to exercise their expertise on the sole terrain where it could have been useful, namely, a patient, careful analysis of the historical documents constituting the dossier of the accused. It is a peculiar situation when one thinks about it. The historians were rarely solicited during the phase of the preliminary investigation, and the few who were never took the stand (with the exception again of Michel Bergès). And yet this preliminary phase is a process of collecting, sorting through, and critiquing various documents. It is, in short, an activity that bears analogies to historical inquiry. On the other hand, these same historians are later called to the stand, with drum rolls for dramatic effect, at the very moment when the judicial process is farthest removed from their practice: the oral debates of a circuit court, in whose halls the weight of legal rhetoric is considerable, a rhetoric unfamiliar to these scholars and impossible for them to master under the circumstances.

Summoned in order to inform the jury about events the latter did not experience, the historians were in fact in much the same situation as their "students": Most of these scholars had not experienced the Vichy period, either. To compound matters, like the jury, they were also among the only ones not to know the contents of the dossier, since it is only open to the magistrates, lawyers, plaintiffs, and defendant.

P.P.: They may not have known the contents of the dossier, but they are nonetheless among the foremost investigators in this historical field. When Robert Paxton takes the stand, it is not as an amateur detective but rather to instruct the court about the period during which these acts occurred.

H.R.: Certainly none of the historians set out to play amateur detective. But, willingly or not, they were hostage to the court's line of questioning: guilty or innocent. With the exceptions of Henri Amouroux[7] and Michel Bergès,[8] who spoke more in favor of the defendant, all of the historians feared that their remarks could strengthen the defense argument, which was a perfectly reasonable fear, particularly at the beginning of the trial. On this count, they were in the same position as most of the witnesses who did not have enough experience to be able to anticipate the consequences that their deposition would have for the course of the trial. This is typical of testimony in circuit court. Moreover, we can even ask ourselves how many lies, well-intentioned or otherwise,

7. Amouroux is a journalist and writer who has published numerous books for the general public on the history of the Occupation. Most notable among these is the ten-volume *Grande histoire des Français sous l'Occupation* (Paris: Robert Laffont, 1976–93), which cannot be considered a scholarly work. Fairly popular, especially among a generation that lived through the war, and having himself experienced the Occupation (he was a journalist in Bordeaux), Amouroux has always given a very moderate vision of Vichy, insisting in particular on the weight of circumstances and the slim margin for maneuver left to Pétain's government. It is for this reason that Amouroux was summoned by Papon to offer arguments in his defense. However, inspired by Robert Paxton's works, a new generation of historians has rejected this thesis. Paxton has demonstrated Vichy's willing collaboration with Germany and the politics of repression and persecution brought to bear on the opposition and the Jews. The chief justice opted to hear Amouroux's deposition right after that of Paxton, in order to present the court with a sort of oppositional debate between historians.

8. Trained in political science, Michel Bergès made his name in 1981 when he discovered documents in Bordeaux's archives that made it possible to implicate Papon. Bergès worked closely with the victims before changing his mind and declaring that the documents did not justify a conviction. More specifically, Bergès defended the idea that nothing in the archives directly incriminated Papon in the deportation of Jews from Bordeaux in 1942–43. Bergès, the only historian who had been able to work closely with the defendant's judicial dossier, was summoned to appear by Papon.

were offered up by all parties concerned during the five months of hearings in Bordeaux. This situation was quite normal, given the circumstances. It turned out to be particularly delicate for the historians who were in the position of experts who were supposed to put forth solid truths when in fact no historical truth could be stated outside of an interpretive framework and a prior line of questioning. The scholars spoke a great deal, for instance, about the collaboration practiced by civil servants; that the historians testified on this matter was quite normal because it concerned a fact—regardless of whether this collaboration was voluntary or accepted and endured without much soul-searching—central to the case. Some of these scholars even contested—and rightly so—the idea that Maurice Papon could have "been aware of the Final Solution" from the very moment he assumed his functions. While their objections were accurate on a historical level, the argument is not necessarily in contradiction with a conviction for crimes against humanity. Even if the French official did not know the true fate of the deported Jews, putting entire families onto trains and subjecting them to horrifying fates, already constitutes a "crime against humanity." On the other hand, the historians did not offer to elaborate on the possible significance of acts of resistance on the part of those same civil servants who had participated in criminal acts, a point of history which turns out to be important for understanding the final stages of the Vichy government and even more for situating the case of the defendant, as we saw later on (and this independently of any value judgment). It has been known for a long time now that, starting in 1943, numerous civil servants began distancing themselves from the Vichy government, either out of opportunism or prudence or because they disagreed with the direction it had taken, controlled increasingly by the most extreme elements of the collaboration. This was the case, for instance, of François Mitterrand, future president of the French Republic, who held a modest position within the Vichy administration but joined the Resistance in 1943 and even took on responsibilities of note. Starting in the summer of 1944, some of the least compromised among the former Vichy civil servants served in General de Gaulle's provisional government the same way they had served Pétain. Some had helped the Resistance, in spite of their official duties. Maurice Papon claimed to have been among these, even if no material proof was ever provided to confirm this assertion. *In the logic of the circuit court but not in that of history*, recalling these facts, which are part of the "context" that historians were supposed to discuss, would have been rendering service to the cause of the defense.

Here is precisely where the gap exists between a case tried in court and one investigated by historians. This is not to claim that historians are any more impartial when they publish scientific works and articles. But the contradiction, argumentation, and refutation of one interpretation or another does not take place with the constraints and pressures found in a court of assizes trying a case considered "historic" (in all senses of the term).

To be frank, I would add that it is fortunate in the long run that historians were not more deeply involved in these proceedings. The appearance of Michel Bergès, the only historian—or political scientist, though the distinction does not matter here—with extensive knowledge of the dossier, demonstrated to the point of caricature the obvious limitations of the cohabitation of history and justice. First of all, there are questions to be asked when a scholar expects his or her work to result in the public or judicial incrimination of an individual. One will recall that this was the case back in 1981 when Bergès made public certain documents, thus sparking the Papon affair. I am not passing judgment on Bergès; I do not know what I would have done had I been in his place, even though one of the historian's duties is to find the right path between the necessary disclosure of the truth and an elementary respect for private individuals. On occasion, the path is quite narrow, especially when the aforementioned individuals are suspected of crimes against humanity. One can ask other questions, too: not so much about the fact that Bergès changed his mind in 1997 and took the position that Papon was being tried unjustly, but about the fact that Bergès criticized the prosecution outside the courtroom and expressed his concerns to the media *before* he gave his own testimony. But here again, can one really blame him, given that some of the plaintiffs' lawyers had shown patent disdain for the rules of justice and the necessary respect for the court? Lastly, one can wonder about the significance of Bergès's expert testimony. It was based on a knowledge of the file that he alone possessed and on his personal interpretation of those materials. From the moment that his remarks no longer served the cause that his interpretation was originally supposed to advance—namely, that of the plaintiffs and the prosecution—*his very presence on the witness stand, as a historian*, was hotly contested, as much by the prosecutor's office as by some of the more serious of the plaintiffs' lawyers who argued that Bergès had confused his role as historian with that of judge.

In other words, the presence of historians on the witness stand was legally admissible only as long as they did not know or talk about the file! If such was not the case, the historian was stigmatized for having encroached on prerogatives that belonged exclusively to the magistrates and lawyers. This rather glaring paradox once more underlines the extent to which the rules and practices of such trials have very little to do with those of scientific research. Moreover, this situation considerably undermined the historians' credibility, because they ended up seeming less like experts and more like character witnesses. In the chronology of the hearings, it is not by chance that the historians were called right after and sometimes at the same time as the aforementioned character witnesses. Furthermore, the historians' depositions, like those of the character witnesses, were quickly forgotten. To proceed accordingly cast a shadow of doubt over their remarks. From the moment that it was the symbolism of their position in the university that was being used, with their expert testimony being limited to broad generalizations, there crept in a risk that their knowledge would be degraded to the level of mere opinion, worthy of respect but without any real bearing on the dossier in question. The situation was all the more damaging given that the historical expert testimony had been presented to the court not as an incidental element but as a central piece of the arguments—which, of course, is hardly astonishing in a trial whose real issue is history itself.

P.P.: Should historians have assisted in the preliminary investigation and, if yes, would you have accepted?

H.R.: If the historians had been more closely involved in the preliminary investigation, some of the objections that I have tried to formulate would perhaps have dissipated. In a certain sense, this is what happened during the preliminary investigation carried out in the Touvier case. Appointed by ecclesiastical authorities and presided over by René Rémond, the expert commission of historians constituted a sort of parallel preliminary investigation, with judges and historians working closely together (even if they appeared to be pursuing different objectives).[9] It is as a result of this cooperative effort that some of these historians were later called to testify in the Touvier trial. Contrary to what occurred in the Papon trial, these historians had extensive knowledge of the Touvier files. But that still does not eliminate the ambiguity of this way of proceeding.

Germany also experienced this situation in the 1960s when the Fed-

9. The ecclesiastical authorities conferred on Rémond the mission of investigating the complicity of the French church in helping hide Paul Touvier. In principle, this commission was not allowed to interfere with the judicial inquiry brought against Touvier; see Rémond et al., *Touvier et l'Église.*

eral Republic decided to resume prosecution of Nazi war criminals. Historians were included very early in the proceedings. They helped collect evidentiary documents which they later used extensively to produce new historical scholarship. This instance differs considerably from the French example. Not only is the German context much more complex (given the weight of the guilt engendered by Nazism and the Holocaust), but the collaboration of jurists and historians also took place at a time when the history of the Nazi period was itself still in the midst of substantial evolution. At the time, this evolution had not reached a degree of maturity sufficient for this history to be able to provide magistrates with tried and true interpretive grids. In other words, jurists and historians were seeking a truth that they helped elaborate *together*, each with their respective methods and objectives.

In the French instance, in the context of the late 1990s, the situation was of an entirely different order. The French justice system used as best it could interpretive models that were developed some time ago by foreign and French historiography on Vichy, and none of the French trials for crimes against humanity helped further *scientific* knowledge of this period (unlike in the case of the German trials, or even that of the Eichmann trial in Jerusalem in 1961).

P.P.: But didn't the Nuremberg trials of Nazi war criminals in 1945 and those of Japanese war criminals in Tokyo in 1946 mark an irreversible break? And isn't there an obvious continuity from Nuremberg to The Hague?

H.R.: The break is important, of course, and it invites us to place trials like that of Maurice Papon in a historical perspective, which has not happened very much.

In the years after the war, for the first time in history, a considerable number of courts, both international (as in the case of Nuremberg and Tokyo) and national (as with the political purges in the countries freed from German occupation), unearthed documents, pondered the nature of the events that had unfolded during the war, and tried to apply new penal categories such as "crime against humanity." In so doing, this first wave of trials offered, in the heat of the moment and in a somewhat haphazard manner, a first narration and interpretation of the events that had just ended with the defeat of the Reich. This unprecedented form of historical narrative *preceded* the first historical analyses, which were in turn based extensively on the documents used in these trials — Nuremberg, especially. As a result, the first historical studies were very strongly influenced by the legal models of interpretation. For example, it is worth noting that one of the points shared by all of the trials of the "first wave"—Nuremberg included—is that they did not place any particular emphasis on the Holocaust, a characteristic echoed by the first historical analyses (in the French context, at least).

The first histories of Vichy—most notably Robert Aron's *Vichy Regime*—used approaches very close to those employed in the trials carried out by the High Court of the Liberation (Haute Cour de la Libération): Was Pétain a traitor, and was Vichy the product of a plot hatched against the Third Republic before the war? The question of anti-Semitism was rarely broached, and when it was, it was only treated marginally, seen for the most part as a consequence solely of the Occupation. Similarly, the first histories of the Holocaust and of Nazism were immersed in the logic of the Nuremberg trials, having made significant use of their extraordinary documentary resources. This explains why historians stressed the Nazis' intent from before the war to exterminate the Jews, in much the same way that a court emphasizes criminal intent or premeditation in order to insist that Auschwitz was contained in National Socialism from its very origin.

During a second stage that began in the 1960s and 1970s, many historians tried to free themselves from this judicial thinking, seeking other means of understanding the event. Robert Paxton broke with the paradigm of a Vichy betrayal in order to bring to light the vast Pétainist political project and its roots within the ranks of France's elite. In Germany, a new school of historical thought called into question the intentionalist model and proposed its own functionalist method. Through the composition of a detailed chronology, this school identified the historical stages that led to the extermination of European Jews. Without choosing sides in a polemic that today is behind us, I would simply like to emphasize the fact that the history of the Occupation in France, much like the general history of Nazism, felt it necessary *to break with the judicial thinking* produced by the first wave of trials in order to move forward. It began making use of other archival collections than those assembled for the postwar trials and offered interpretive models that stem from the protocols of historical studies and not legal or political domains.

At this juncture, a third stage intervenes. As unprecedented as the first judicial wave, it could be termed a second purge. In Germany at the end of the 1950s, and in France during the early 1980s, a new wave of legal proceedings was set in motion. For France, it took place decades after the events, beginning with the preliminary investigations brought against Jean Leguay, indicted in 1979 but deceased before going to trial, and his immediate superior, René Bousquet, indicted in 1991 and assassinated in 1993. It crystalized around the Touvier and Papon trials in 1994 and 1997–98, respectively. The Barbie trial in 1987 also belonged to this stage, though it was informed by a different punitive logic, since by definition the purge was aimed solely at French suspects. This second purge was based on charges that were now only taking into account the question of anti-Semitic persecutions. Given the belated character of these trials, given the fact that the historiography of the period had evolved considerably since the 1970s (especially the historiography concerning Vichy), the magistrates found themselves able to draw on partly established historical knowledge but no longer in a position to generate it themselves.

P.P.: What do you think of the role played by Serge Klarsfeld?

H.R.: He is emblematic of the process I am describing here. Without any doubt, he has rendered significant services to historical knowledge and contributed greatly to the reawakening of memory. But the constant objective for him has been to bring to justice officials who escaped the purge or were never tried for the roles they had in the Holocaust. And despite what he may have said himself, he has set out to be the armed wing of a form of vengeance. In light of his attitude and that of his son Arno during the Papon trial, one wonders to what extent he tried to force the hand of the court and lead it to write the history he hoped to see written, with a verdict that would be the most justified in his eyes, neither acquittal nor a maximum sentence, in order to respect a hierarchy consisting of Barbie, Touvier, and Papon. On a historical level, it was not without some foundation. But was it justified or acceptable on juridical and judicial grounds? It is in this sense that the remark by Hannah Arendt that you cited earlier finds its fullest meaning. One cannot ask for justice, mobilize a court, jury, and lawyers, and at the same time behave as if a particular verdict is the only solution—unless one sees the justice system as but an instrument of vengeance and an almost accessory mechanism with respect to the objective pursued. At a time when questions were once again being asked about the justice system's independence, Klarsfeld's approach was rather unfortunate.

This commingling of vengeance and justice, memory and history, has never troubled Serge Klarsfeld; he has embraced it from the beginning. For scholars, the problem is quite different. How should they handle the fact that in a certain sense these belated trials were made possible by the progress of historical knowledge? How could they prevent the justice system from trying to instrumentalize those same historians who had been the catalysts for an evolution in our knowledge? Granted, these cases were submitted to the Justice Department quite promptly: as early as 1973 for the first complaints filed and as early as 1979 for the first indictment—that is, at the moment when another history of the period was being written, one that served in part to inspire it. But in the case of the actual trials themselves (especially that of Papon, which took place quite some time later), the historical knowledge at issue was already well established, and the court never sought to propose an interpretive model that differed from that of the historians. It simply caricatured certain historical interpretations. In so doing, it placed historians in a difficult position, since none of the scholars summoned to appear in court—except perhaps Michel Bergès—had ever considered themselves potential auxiliaries of the Justice Department. Similarly, with the exception of the study cited above concerning Touvier and the church, none of their research had originated in a mission to produce court evidence.

It is an extremely ambiguous situation and constitutes one more reason for my refusal to testify, especially given the work that I have performed on my own. Since I have gone in the direction of studying the history of the memory of Vichy, the Papon trial was for me an opportunity for research and reflection. Under no circumstances did I want the lines of inquiry to which this trial might lead me to be formulated in the middle of a hearing and used to judge or convict an individual. I have on occasion helped a magistrate or investigator find his or her way through bibliographies and archives concerning the period. But even if I had agreed to help in this instance, I probably would have refused to participate directly in the preliminary investigations. As a matter of fact, I strongly believe in the separation of roles and domains of knowledge, even if the boundaries are not airtight between judicial and historical knowledge. I must add that this problem is marginal and exceptional. Certainly, it has fostered reflection on the nature of historical work. It has also reignited discussion about the ambiguous relations existing between the justice system and history. These questions, however, should only preoccupy a handful of World War II historians—unless one is of the opinion that the history of the entire twentieth century must be written in the courtroom.

P.P.: From your perspective as a historian (and not as a citizen), should the Papon trial have taken place, fifty years after the fact?

H.R.: One cannot give a cut-and-dried answer to this question. Once the courts had been called into the matter, they had to see it through to the end. Even if some of the reasons given were not without some legitimacy, the fact that those in power placed obstacles in the way of these proceedings was disastrous on moral and judicial levels. This was particularly true during Mitterrand's presidency. In my opinion, it would have been better to reopen a national debate on the viability of trying individuals so long after the fact. I do not know if this was possible politically or legally. The parliamentary debates that took place in December 1964 prior to the vote on the imprescriptibility of crimes against humanity failed to elicit any public interest, and no one foresaw the political, legal, and moral consequences of such a decision. At that time, all the protagonists had their eyes set on Nazi criminals who were in hiding (like Klaus Barbie), and nobody had imagined that this law could serve as a fulcrum to enable a second purge in France against French officials from the Vichy government. People only realized this much later, even well after the first steps taken in 1973 to draw on this imprescriptibility, after Touvier's presidential pardon from Georges Pompidou. While historical awareness has continued to grow since the 1970s and the duty to remember has become an ever more invasive injunction, the slowness of the judicial procedures only intensified the need for justice, which in the end led to these belated trials. Under such conditions, a dismissal would certainly not have been understood, the precedent of Touvier's previous acquittal by the Paris Court of Appeals on April 13, 1992, having aroused considerable emotion (and justifiably so).[10] Once the machine was set in motion, these trials were inevitable, if only with respect to the workings of the justice system. The question becomes one of examining how these trials unfold and evaluating their significance and meaning.

In this respect, as a historian and as a citizen, I would first set apart the only gain that strikes me as unquestionable in these proceedings: They have made it possible to refine the notion of "crimes against humanity" and to give it real substance, not just on a juridical level but in cultural and political terms as well. The only real victory for those who wanted these belated trials is the fact that after the war in the former Yugoslavia an international tribunal was convened and was able to function without waiting for the problems that the absence of prescription by definition engenders. It is in this sense that imprescriptibility on a legal level strikes me as a problem. It is better to try the criminals as quickly as

---

10. Charges were renewed against Touvier on November 27 of the same year when the Criminal Chamber of the High Court of Appeals reversed part of the acquittal. Trans.

possible than to give them the time to slip off secretively into the forgotten realms of history, realms from which it is very difficult, and in the long run hardly desirable, to uproot them. Similarly, with respect to the victims and their descendants, if they feel that justice has been done, I have nothing to add.

Moreover, as I have been saying for quite some time, these trials have not contributed in any way to a better scientific knowledge of the period. Quite the contrary. At best, they have perhaps sensitized public opinion, and even here we must each judge for ourselves. Do we have to stage such trials in order to give the population history lessons? What will we do in the future? We sometimes lose sight of the fact that the role of a trial is to contribute to an anamnesis: It has been judged in court and is now over and done with. Yet this closure is unbearable from the perspective of the duty to remember such as it is understood today. With this in mind, what will the next stage be and in what way will the stakes be raised again?

P.P.: After the Papon trial, will Vichy thus be a past "that has passed"?

H.R.: I very much doubt it, even if sometimes I find this quite regrettable—not out of a criminal desire for forgetfulness but because I am convinced that the religion of memory and the obsession with the past lead to a sort of impasse, as I've said elsewhere. For me, accepting the past and its burdens means living with the uncertainty that is passed on to us. The dilemmas that could not be resolved in their time must remain unresolved in memory and for posterity. We cannot retrospectively answer with certainty the question of whether the true political legitimacy between 1940 and 1944 was in Vichy with Pétain, in London with de Gaulle, or in the hills of Vercors with the interior Resistance. We can only offer statements of personal conviction. Yes, for myself, as for the majority of the French population today, legitimacy was with de Gaulle and the Resistance. Of course, it is rather easy to adopt this stance today. But even if it is in the name of a respectable political morality, by denying Vichy's legitimacy (albeit de facto), I fall into the trap of "resistancialism" that the duty to remember has been fighting against for the past thirty years. The schisms of the day, the existence of one or several Frances, cannot be erased with the stroke of a judicial pen. Though glaring in retrospect, the problems posed by the postwar purge and its imperfections cannot be fixed fifty years later. Re-creating them in an anachronistic context lacking any notion of urgency or political and moral reconstruction will not resolve anything. What France is having a difficult time accepting today is not so much its past but the fact that it must live with a rupture that no trial, commemoration, or speech can redress. In my opinion, the real issue for our generation and future ones is to face and accept the irreparable.

P.P.: You agree then with Hannah Arendt: yes, for the judgment of a person; no, for the judgment of a regime or human nature.

H.R.: Yes, though neither one nor the other was carried out properly in the Papon trial. France found itself caught up in an unprecedented dilemma as soon as a real court was convened again. Can anyone seriously deny that history has condemned the Vichy government? All of the opinion polls, especially those carried out at the beginning of the trial, show the extent to which the majority of the French—nearly 75 percent—agree that this government and those who served it stand as one of the darkest moments in French history. A great majority condemn this government for its persecution of Jews and the role, clearly established for more than twenty years now, that it played in the application of the Final Solution in France. Since the end of the war, public opinion has never been so unanimous in its stance against Vichy, nor have the grounds on which we judge it morally ever been so clear with respect to the central importance of the question of the Holocaust. Even the existence of a minority sympathetic to the National Front, indulgent or even enthusiastic with respect to Vichy, cannot overshadow this evolution, quite evident in the fifty years since the war.

This means that the general awakening to these issues was real, even if it was not at all final or ideal. It means that "history as the world's court of judgment" has reached its verdict, independently of the real courts, which came into the picture well after this national awakening. I do not agree that it took the crimes against humanity trials of French citizens for this awakening of consciences to occur. The trials did contribute to a certain sensitization, but of what sort? The claim simply cannot be defended that prior to 1994 (the date of the Touvier trial) and even prior to the 1980s (the period when the procedures began) the French were living in complete denial or were subject to a culpable indulgence toward the Vichy regime.

Personally, I feel that there was something incongruous about reopening one or several cases. It gave the impression, obvious during the Papon trial, that it was necessary once more to examine a dossier that was already largely settled in the public's mind. With the slow and difficult study of an individual case, we ran the risk of raising new doubts when many of the answers were already satisfactory. In the context of the purge, none of the cases was exemplary on its own. Rather, it was the sum of the cases investigated that provided meaning and gave an ample idea of what the collaboration and Pétainism had been (even if that idea was limited to the issues of the day). A half century later, in the minds of many, Maurice Papon was supposed to represent, *by himself*, an entire era and government. But because his case was complicated, isolated, and addressed long after the fact, the questions it provoked marked a sort of regression in historical knowledge once they took on an exemplary status that was overmediatized and overexploited. Moreover, to assert, without showing any formal proof, that the defendant knew about the Final Solution as early as June 1942 (according to the indictment) made many uncomfortable, as if the problem in that era had been as simple as legal rhetoric would have it (i.e., he either did or did not know). In adopting this stance, the prosecution overlooked the possible intermediate attitudes as well as the very real difficulty of answering such a question with certainty; it is, in fact, nearly impossible to do so. Similarly, denying Papon's contributions to the Resistance—as the prosecution did—also created confusion in the public's mind when legitimate figures from the French Resistance came to testify in his favor. How could one be, the argument went, both a cog in the administrative wheel that orchestrated the persecution of Jews *and* a member of the Resistance against the occupying power? The answer, of course, has been known for quite some time. A great many Vichy civil servants went from loyalty to the Pétain government to dissidence and later to joining the Resistance: This is François Mitterrand's trajectory, for instance. Independently of the moral judgment we might hold on such attitudes, this pattern shows us the porous nature of the government and the composite nature of the Resistance. It is for this very reason that it is risky to use Maurice Papon as an exemplary case before the courts. If he ended up being acquitted or received a light sentence, would this mean that Vichy was acquitted or partially relieved of responsibility? Moreover, the exemplary nature of this case, debatable to begin with, contained other risks due to the trial's circumstances. Could one really argue that the crimes committed under Papon's authority during the Algerian War constituted a form of repeat offense, coming on the heels of those committed during the Occupation? This was the impression conveyed during the hearings in Bordeaux by those caught up in the logic of the assizes. Papon clearly represents a rather remarkable form of administrative continuity (though not without precedent). But what about his superiors, those who gave the orders or covered them up? Should we draw a parallel between the Jewish roundups in 1942–

44 and the Algerian massacres in 1961 and thus between Pétain and de Gaulle? This would be absurd. Perhaps I am too pessimistic, but my impression is that after all this confusion historians will have to start over again on a project of education and explanation that they have every right to believe was already well on its way to fruition—though they would probably have been wrong on this last count.

P.P.: Let's return to the Aubrac affair. As a sort of epilogue to the *Libération* roundtable, historian and Resistance veteran Jean-Pierre Vernant declared, "Experience has taught me that, in the course of historic events, in the behavior of men or in their motives (our own included), there are questions that we ask ourselves, perhaps even about ourselves, where we cannot make up our minds, and where the answer is, 'I don't know.' " What did you learn or "unlearn" through your participation in this roundtable discussion? Do you have the impression that you participated in the symbolic execution of a couple who had been important figures in the Resistance?

H.R.: If there was an execution, it was of a certain memory of the Resistance. Still widespread in France, it prefers legend to truth, sacred history to critical history. But I am quite ready when need be to recognize the inherent limits to any quest for the truth. To a certain degree, this is in fact the conclusion I reached concerning this affair and expressed in the July 11, 1997, issue of *Libération*.

Let us briefly recall the context of this roundtable discussion. It was organized at the express wish of Raymond Aubrac, who had been seriously called into question in a sensationalist work written by historian and journalist Gérard Chauvy, *Aubrac, Lyon 1943*.[11] One of Chauvy's principal sources was Klaus Barbie's testament, a long document with very little credibility that was probably drafted by his lawyer, Vergès, at the time of Barbie's trial in 1987. This text accuses Raymond Aubrac of betraying the Resistance and making possible on June 21, 1943, in Caluire the arrest of Jean Moulin, along with other important figures from the Resistance, including Raymond Aubrac himself. One has to keep in mind that this episode is one of the most controversial in the entire history of the French Resistance. It has sparked polemics on a great number of occasions over the last fifty years. Moreover, the most recent developments have not contributed anything new to the facts or the accusations, these latter being groundless until proof to the con-

---

11. Chauvy's book (Paris: Albin Michel, 1997) includes a preface by Resistance veteran René Fallas, whom Raymond Aubrac sued for libel.

trary is provided. Gérard Chauvy also made use of a judicial dossier assembled by the examining magistrate, Jacques Hamy, when new charges were filed against Barbie after his trial in 1987, a dossier which contains numerous documents regarding the history of the Resistance in 1943 and 1944.

These documents had not been published, but their content was known: Raymond Aubrac himself had circulated them in 1989 (the Barbie text among them) when he was already the target of the campaign led by Vergès. In the context of the Barbie trial and its aftermath, few historians had thought or desired at the time to examine these documents more closely. Chauvy was thus one of the first to make extensive use of them. We can grant him credit for that, but we can also fault him with having failed to maintain a sufficiently critical distance in his use of these documents, employed primarily to cast a shadow of doubt over Raymond Aubrac's loyalty to his comrades. As part of his argument, Chauvy noted contradictions in Raymond Aubrac's description of the circumstances of his arrests (which Judge Hamy had previously done when he took down Raymond Aubrac's deposition). It is true that Aubrac was first arrested in March 1943, at which time he was granted a conditional release. He was arrested a second time on June 21, 1943, with Jean Moulin. Thanks to a group of Resistance partisans led by his wife, Lucie Aubrac, he managed to escape under particularly dangerous circumstances in October 1943. Of the statements in question, some had been made in 1944, mostly in London and then Algiers—and thus in the heat of the moment—while others were made a long time after the fact, most notably in his *Mémoires*, which appeared in 1996.

Raymond Aubrac called for a roundtable discussion to be organized by *Libération* because he wanted the "specialists" to be able to give their opinions of this affair. The roundtable meeting lasted a full day and took place May 17, 1997, in the main offices of *Libération*. On July 9, 1997, more than seven weeks later, the discussions were published almost in their entirety in the form of a supplement that clearly signaled its exceptional nature (through its layout, photographs, etc.). During this seven-week phase of gestation, the various protagonists partly amended and clarified their oral interventions, and it was at this stage that the conflicts were the most heated. This discord is apparent when one reads the series of articles published in *Libération* on July 9, 1997, in which the protagonists give their impressions of both the form and content of the debates.

In addition to Lucie and Raymond Aubrac, the roundtable brought together several historians—Maurice Agulhon, Jean-Pierre Azéma, François Bédarida, Laurent Douzou, Dominique Veillon, and myself—as well as two other renowned veterans of the Resistance, Jean-Pierre Vernant and Daniel Cordier. Two journalists from *Libération*, Béatrice Vallaeys and Antoine de Gaudemar, moderated the roundtable and its participants later published their impressions in *Libération*'s special supplements (see Bibliography).

Once in print, the roundtable provoked rather lively polemics. Some historians, including a few of those who had agreed to participate in the roundtable, publicly reproached their colleagues with having indulged in a "deplorable history lesson," played "inquisitor," poorly studied the case, and asked scandalous, even shameful, questions. Their primary target was a question asked by Daniel Cordier, who is a Resistance veteran rather than a scholar. The question touched on the arrest of Raymond Aubrac's parents, which occurred in December 1943, after his escape. Cordier wanted to know if there could be any link between this arrest, which resulted in the deportation of his parents and their demise in the death camps, and the possibility that the Nazis might have, by one means or another, uncovered the true identity of the younger Aubrac couple. The question thus was not gratuitous with respect to the case, even if it might seem offensive.

After some lengthy exchanges, on occasion tense but never uncivil, three points emerged—at least, from my point of view. First, the accusation of betrayal did not hold water and was in truth disgraceful. This was stated explicitly on several occasions and by all of the participants. Second, it was difficult not to notice that Raymond Aubrac had indeed contradicted himself several times concerning the circumstances of his detention and that, speaking many years later, some of his comrades had also made inaccurate statements on important issues, such as the proven fact that the Gestapo in Lyon knew that it had captured "Aubrac," the pseudonym of a high-ranking member of the clandestine Resistance. Third, Lucie Aubrac admitted a number of times that the accounts she gave in her books about her attempts to free Raymond Aubrac after his first arrest in March 1943 and of the successful escape in October 1943 contained liberties with the truth scattered here and there, due (in her own words) to her tendency to spin tales.

P.P.: How do you interpret the criticisms that were made of this round-table?

H.R.: First of all, it is important to specify that this roundtable did not elicit only criticism, even if the criticisms were the most visible. One should note that the criticisms addressed several aspects of the round-table: the facts themselves, the nature of the questions asked, the desirability of such a procedure, and the organization or even the principle of such a roundtable.

Where the facts are concerned, without going into the details of this complex affair, I for my part can only repeat what I said and wrote at the time of the roundtable. On the one hand, based on the documents, the notion of a betrayal strikes me as unfounded. On the other hand, I merely noted that Raymond Aubrac had made contradictory statements, a fact which had been generally acknowledged before the roundtable. In the absence of other proofs, and given Raymond Aubrac's statement that he could not explain the contradictions, I decided to refrain from drawing any conclusions whatsoever.

The rest is another matter. I was astonished, for instance, by the violence of some of the criticisms and by the fact that close colleagues spoke publicly without first seeking more information or by seeking it only from the Aubracs. This way of proceeding effectively condemned a number of their colleagues who had participated in the roundtable— myself included—without any chance for appeal or even a hearing. The metaphor of the tribunal, which these same colleagues deplored, had been turned around and was now working against us. I think that this rather partial attitude was due to the fact that Lucie and Raymond Aubrac, by their very popularity and fame, were considered untouchable, even by professional historians, and this in spite of the questions that their itineraries might suggest to historians. Although this aspect was not mentioned by any of the historians present at the roundtable (in passing or explicitly), because the Aubracs had been sympathetic to the Communist Party—especially Raymond Aubrac, very committed to the Communist International after the war—examining their stories was taboo. It was seen as an act of "flagrant anticommunism" or, worse yet, as tearing down legends today deemed necessary. When Daniel Cordier revealed a few years ago that another great veteran of the Resistance, Henri Frenay, known on the contrary for his fierce anticommunism, had been a die-hard follower of Pétain in 1940, only the Resistance circles had reacted. Historians, including some of those who came out against the May 1997 roundtable, had strongly supported Cordier's approach and analyses; Cordier's findings, quite simply, had been shown to be historically accurate. Why would potentially upsetting investigations be more legitimate when focused on Resistance veterans from the Right than from the Left? Moreover, the argument of the "necessary myth," especially when invoked by scholars or intellectuals, leaves me incredulous. It is precisely through a refusal to endorse necessary myths that a new perception of the Occupation period was able to take shape in the 1970s. This is the very argument used by authorities from 1971 to 1981 to justify not showing *The Sorrow and the Pity* on French television. On the contrary, the memory of the Resistance has everything to gain from accepting the critical eye of historians. Perhaps this will be at the cost of tarnishing a few individuals' reputations, or it will cause us to be more circumspect with respect to the tales of Resistance veterans. Perhaps it will lead us to break out of the habit of seeing particular heroes as being, in and of themselves, representative of the entire Resistance, which was, after all, pluralist and very much divided along ideological lines. But I do not really see where the Resistance, the universal project that it represented, the ideal of liberty that it defended, would have anything to fear from a critical eye cast on some of its members. Similarly, in all naïveté, I believe that the duty to truthfulness is very much part of the ideal of the Resistance, which fought the war against lies.

P.P.: Everything depends on what one means by "truth." I understand truth as a process, not as an isolated fact. Does a historian identify facts or an event as being accurate?

H.R.: Granted, establishing the truth is a process. But the gas chambers existed. Regardless of the process used to arrive at this statement of the obvious, we must still affirm that it is factually correct. Along the same lines, truth and lies are not diluted by this process. One can list all the nuances possible, take all the methodological precautions necessary, but in the end this is not the same thing as saying that one person betrayed his or her comrades and that another did not. Why should it be considered perfectly legitimate to assert as true, based on the existing documents, that Raymond Aubrac never betrayed his comrades in Caluire while, on the other hand, it would be judged disgraceful to point out the clear contradictions in his statements—especially if one is not claiming that these contradictions are the product of guilty acts?

On this point, I reject the argument that historians should not allow themselves to judge agents of history. We have now come full circle to my point of departure. If these agents, themselves witnesses as well, are my contemporaries, and if my judgment addresses *not their past acts but their statements made today*, then I do not see any reason why I should consider them as not responsible and possessing a right to do and say as they please, simply because they are genuine heroes of the Resistance. I never put forth any judgment whatsoever concerning the behavior of Lucie or Raymond Aubrac *during* the war, and any judgments of their remarks should be open to disagreement and offered *outside of any tribunal or grand jury* (and the roundtable was not a tribunal, even if the Resistance veterans who requested it may have imagined it in those terms). After all, studying the fragile nature of witnesses's accounts as a historian does not prevent me from contesting, as a citizen, *current* statements from a Resistance veteran who claims to be defending a duty to remember while at the same time explaining that she reserves the right to take liberties with historical truth. Although Lucie Aubrac deserves all of our respect for her activities in 1943, she cannot refuse to allow a historian to disagree with her current conception of the memory of the Resistance, especially since she has never stopped stating that the witnesses alone possess the historical truth and that historians can never understand anything about the experience of the Resistance.[12] It is a natural tendency for some agents of history to adopt this attitude toward historians of the present, and it is one of the risks of the craft. Historians must resist it, whatever the price may be.

In truth, the heart of the problem lies in the role that the Aubracs wanted historians to play. The historians had been invited to be candid in their questions — "American style" in Raymond Aubrac's words (cf. the introduction to the roundtable publication). This is entirely to his credit. However, the Resistance veterans slandered in this affair thought that they could use the professional legitimacy of the scholars participating to extract themselves from an unpleasant situation. They made the mistake of thinking that it would be easy to intimidate and instrumentalize historians who were going to be put in an awkward position. Avoiding the sensitive subjects when these had already been the object of public debate for months would have been to make fools of ourselves and to give the appearance of being predisposed to the Aubracs' view. But if we chose to touch on these subjects, it meant that we were pushing the discussion to its limits, with the risk of appearing to be inquisitors — which, of course, is what happened.

P.P.: What lessons do you draw from this?

H.R.: I do not regret having participated in this roundtable, even if it was not easy for anyone. But I probably will not undertake such an exercise again if the historical stakes, properly speaking, are as slight. For me, if the hypothesis of a betrayal is rejected, the rest—Raymond

---

12. Unless, of course, the actor in question "guides" the historian's pen or keeps a "hawklike eye" on their work, as Pierre Laborie so rightly observed.

Aubrac's contradictory statements and Lucie Aubrac's liberties with the truth—do not merit all this attention from historians. If I agreed to participate in the discussion in spite of this, it was in order to resolve a problem that historians of the present encounter when polemics of this nature break out. To keep silent on the dispute generated by the publication of Gérard Chauvy's work would be to become an accomplice of essentially unfounded accusations. One must remember, moreover, that Raymond Aubrac had repeatedly insisted that the recognized specialists of the Resistance make their positions known on this question, as they had done on other occasions—most notably, when a journalist practicing "investigative history" accused Jean Moulin, with no proof whatsoever, of having been a Soviet agent.[13] Intervening in these polemics, insofar as they are debates marked by a degree of urgency, means running the risk of not being able to control one's discourse, of not being understood. In this respect, the most warranted criticism concerning the roundtable meeting lies not in decrying the principle but in regretting its logistics. Was a large-circulation daily paper the most appropriate host for such an encounter? Perhaps not. But in that case all of the participants bear part of the blame. Even if *Libération* did respect the wishes and statements of all the participants, it is evident that the paper tried to create a big media splash: This is the nature of journalism. Raymond Aubrac called for this meeting and, given the public nature of the polemic, he quite naturally wanted to give the roundtable substantial publicity. But why later insult the historians who lent themselves to this difficult exercise once the results failed to measure up to his expectations? The historians invited to the discussion who were close to the Aubracs basically kept silent throughout the meeting. Why yield later to pressure and declare that the meeting had been scandalous? Why not continue to remain silent? The other historians—those of us who were called into question—accepted this roundtable discussion because it enabled us to take positions publicly and thus break our supposedly complicitous silence. Unquestionably, all of us underestimated the impact of such a publication and the effects on people's images that it would produce (in one direction as in the other). For the reasons explained above, we were swept up in a dynamic in which it was difficult to remain calm and detached.

13. Thierry Wolton, *Le grand recrutement* (Paris: Grasset, 1993). For the refutations, see Pierre Vidal-Naquet, *Le trait empoisonné*; Jean-Pierre Azéma, François Bédarida, and Robert Frank, eds., *Jean Moulin et la Résistance en 1943*; and Conan and Rousso, *Vichy: An Ever-Present Past.*

P.P.: Were all of the questions fair?

H.R.: We were criticized for having asked the question about Raymond Aubrac's parents and especially for having published it. On this point, I readily acknowledge that the question was indelicate and doubtless touched on a limit that historians must avoid transgressing, for reasons tied mostly to respect for individuals, the tragic occurrences they experience, and their personal suffering (though not all of the participants in the roundtable necessarily saw it this way). But aside from the fact that it was not a historian but rather Daniel Cordier, a *veteran of the Resistance* and thus a peer, the Aubracs' equal, who put this question on the table, it should also be known that some of us did request that the question not appear in the publication, a request that Cordier willingly granted, even though one can imagine that the answer to this question had its importance for understanding the details of the facts. *It is Lucie Aubrac herself who steadfastly refused to withdraw this question from the printed text,* having understood all of the benefit she could draw from it. Thanks to this question which "went too far," the two Resistance veterans could appear primarily as victims. This shows the extent to which a power struggle had progressively set in, not only during the roundtable itself, but during the seven weeks that preceded the publication of the discussions. Lucie and Raymond Aubrac had realized that this publication was not going to be to their advantage, and the historians had become irritated at seeing themselves treated as mere foils.

The power struggle broke out initially among the Resistance veterans. Each of them was defending a different conception of the memory of the Resistance: On one side, Daniel Cordier was the tireless defender of painstaking historical exactitude, while Lucie Aubrac preferred her penchant for spinning tales. Then, during the roundtable, it was time for old quarrels to flare up. Dating back to the Occupation, these well-known quarrels opposed the interior Resistance, represented here by the Aubracs, to the representatives of General de Gaulle and the exterior Resistance, among whom Cordier is today an emblematic figure. Lastly, as if by projection, another power struggle appeared, one that pitted the Aubracs against some of the participating historians. The instrumentalization of historical knowledge had failed and the usual conflict that characterizes the relations between witnesses and historians had lost its friendly aspect and become more contentious. In the final analysis, we fell into a multileveled trap whose control ultimately escaped us all.

P.P.: Looking beyond the Aubrac affair, do you think that the legacy of the Resistance is threatened today? If so, do you find this worrisome?

H.R.: Yes, it probably is threatened. Like other historians working on this period, I formulated this hypothesis a fair while ago. It is important, however, to be clear about our terms. I do not believe that the image of the Resistance is threatened by historical examination in and of itself. Its memory is problematic today for other reasons.

The primary culprit lies in the ideological attacks, like those plaguing the memory of Jean Moulin for decades now. This is partly a consequence of the ongoing reevaluation of the history of communism (and thus of antifascism as well), along the lines of François Furet's work in *The Passing of an Illusion.* This is an entirely different debate, asking from a moral point of view how we can make a political legacy fruitful while leaving aside its negative aspects. On this question, I do not share Furet's view that the unilateral condemnation of antifascism was the lever that triggered the rise of international communism during the 1930s and 1940s, but I do agree completely with the idea that it is necessary to draw up a critical, unflinching account that would provide— if such a thing is possible, and as one would do for other events—a historical analysis of political morality.

Lastly, another argument is needed to explain the current situation of the memory of the Resistance. In my opinion, the historians and former members of the Resistance who set out to write histories are very much mistaken if they believe that they must also aim to preserve its edifying value. Even if I find fault with this approach, I can understand it on the part of the agents. I find it less excusable on the part of intellectuals or scholars. One does not write history with the goal of defending a particular set of values. The writing of history, a free and critical writing that restores the breadth and complexity of the past, is a value in itself and merits defending.

We are faced with two options. On the one hand, if a given episode of the past contains universal significance—which is the case for the Resistance commitment—then there is no need for a historical narrative to depict it. To do so is to risk writing a mythological history, oriented toward certain ends in a most suspect manner. We risk betraying the facts through the same sort of excesses that we see today with the duty to remember. Paradoxically, in acting as if the legacy of the event were not sufficient in and of itself, we end up weakening it through the very fact of seeking to defend it with slanted information. The other possibility is that the event no longer has any value for contemporaries, in which case it is entirely misguided to try to re-create it artificially. In any case, it is not the role of the historian to be an evangelist, an attitude which to my mind is as objectionable as that of judge or prosecutor.

At the risk of seeming idealist myself, I believe that we should let history be the judge, all the while keeping in mind the duty to truthfulness and the duty to knowledge which is indissociable from it. The legacy of the French and foreign opposition to Nazism and fascism does not need defending today, nor does Vichy need to be summoned before a court born of today's preoccupations. The Resistance has won the battle for posterity quite handily and it has imbued our democratic societies with its ideals, ideals which go much further back in time than World War II. Vichy has clearly been defeated by history, and there is no need to build it back up into an imaginary adversary with the sole objective of comforting ideological postures announcing themselves anachronistically as antifascist.

If new dangers threaten, rather than resuscitate ghosts we should invent new forms of action and resistance that will enable us to face the battles of today and tomorrow. An ethical necessity, historical truth remains in this context an indispensable weapon. The tensions and uncertainties that it bears, which are a reflection of humankind's incompletion, must lead us to knowledge and not to faith. The transmission of the past must not be limited to the cult of heroes and victims.

Appendix

Letter from Henry Rousso to the
Presiding Chief Justice, Bordeaux

Paris, October 6, 1997
Chief Justice of the Court of Assizes
Palais de Justice
Place de la République
33077 Bordeaux Cedex

Dear Chief Justice,

I have been summoned to appear as a witness at the request of Maurice Papon, currently indicted for complicity in crimes against humanity. I became aware of this request first via the press, without the petitioner or his legal counsel having given me prior notification of their intentions. I find questionable the public use of my name and status as historian.

With all due respect to the court, I wish not to testify for the following reasons.

I would first like to invoke ethical grounds and a question of principle. On the occasion of another trial for crimes against humanity (that of Paul Touvier), I wrote that to my mind the presence of historians within a court of assizes poses a number of problems. It was because of this opinion that I had declined the invitation from plaintiffs who wanted to petition the Court of Versailles for my testimony. It thus strikes me as impossible to comply today with Maurice Papon's request when I just recently turned down plaintiffs from an earlier trial.

In my soul and conscience, I believe that historians cannot be "witnesses" and that a role as "expert witness" rather poorly suits the rules and objectives of a court trial. It is one thing to try to understand history in the context of a research project or course lesson, with the intellectual freedom that such activities presuppose; it is quite another to try to do so under oath when an individual's fate hangs in the balance. I would like to add that these views are of a strictly personal nature. In no way do they imply an opinion concerning the participation of other historians at this trial, whether they be summoned at the behest of the prosecutor, the plaintiffs, or the defense.

Lastly, having been summoned against my will, in a publicized manner that I find deplorable, and not having moreover any direct tie to the acts at issue, I very much fear that my "testimony" is only a pretext for an instrumentalization of scientific research and historical interpretations, elaborated and formulated in contexts other than that of the court of assizes. Once again, the argumentation developed in a trial is not of the same nature as that produced by scholars.

I would be most grateful if the court would take into consideration these reasons.

Most sincerely,
Henry Rousso, Research Director, CNRS
Director, Institute of the History of the Present

French Legal Procedure and Terms

French legal procedure is very different from American procedure. It is not based on the principle of cross-examination. The court of assizes is responsible for trying the most serious crimes and is composed of a nine-member jury (drawn at random from the general population) and three magistrates. The twelve members of the court, the magistrates included, participate in the final deliberations and deliver a verdict. No justification accompanies the verdict, and the decision cannot be appealed.[1] The only possible recourse is to go before the highest court in France, the Supreme Court of Appeals. It rules only on whether the trial proceedings were in conformity with the law; it does not address the actual content of the case.

Before being brought before the court, the accused is taken into custody and interviewed by an independent examining magistrate, who is the only one empowered to carry out investigations (with the help of the Criminal Investigation Department). This phase of the preliminary investigation, known as the "examination," leads either to the charges being dismissed or to the case being sent on to the court, once the case has been examined by another body, the Court of Criminal Appeal. The Court of Criminal Appeal issues a referral ruling, which identifies the precise actions with which the accused is being charged and the accusations on which he or she is going to be judged. The court of assizes cannot stray from the charges named in the referral ruling.

In an assizes trial, the accused, presumed innocent, is subjected to

1. This changed in 2000 with the application of a new law.

interrogation throughout the proceedings and has a legal right to lie, since he or she is not required to be sworn in. The witnesses can be summoned by the prosecuting attorney, plaintiffs, or defense. Normally, it is not possible to refuse to testify unless the chief justice allows otherwise (as in Rousso's case). Once on the stand, witnesses swear under oath to "tell the truth, the whole truth and nothing but the truth" and to "speak without hatred or fear" (to quote the official formula). The witnesses' status is the same, regardless of which party called them. Witnesses can be questioned by the party who called them to the stand, by the prosecutor, the defense lawyers, or the plaintiffs, or by the accused, who is always given the last word. In principle, when witnesses give their testimony, they should always address the chief presiding judge and not the person who questioned them. The historians who testified during the Papon trial were, legally speaking, witnesses just like the others. It is also important to understand that the French legal process is based on a principle of oral debate. Witnesses do not have the right to read notes or use any other written document. Moreover, there is no official transcript of the trial. On an extremely exceptional basis, the entirety of the debates can be recorded on video (as in the Barbie and Touvier trials for crimes against humanity), but in principle these tapes cannot be consulted for twenty years.[2]

Lastly, it is important to keep in mind that in French law, crimes against humanity are the only crimes for which there exists no statute of limitations, that is, deadline limits for the prosecution of ten, twenty, or thirty years after the crime, depending on its nature. This exceptional status dates from a law approved in 1964 which argued that crimes against humanity are "imprescriptible by nature." It was, of course, intended exclusively to allow the prosecution of crimes committed during World War II.

2. In October 2000, the French cable channel Histoire was allowed to air approximately 70 hours (out of 180) of the Barbie trial, with Henry Rousso serving as historical adviser for the production. This broadcast was considered a significant event in France. Trans.

Selected Bibliography

Arendt, Hannah. *Eichmann in Jerusalem: A Report on the Banality of Evil*. New York: Penguin Books, 1963, 1976.

Aron, Raymond. *Dimensions de la conscience historique*. Paris: Plon, 1961.

———. *Leçons sur l'histoire*. Intro. Sylvie Mesure. Paris: Éditions de Fallois, 1989.

Aron, Robert. *Histoire de Vichy, 1940-1944*. Paris: Arthème Fayard, 1954.

The Vichy Regime, 1940-44. Trans. Humphrey Hare. New York: Macmillan, 1958.

Les Aubrac et les historiens. Special supplements to *Libération*, July 9-13, 1997. The unabridged texts in electronic form are available at http://www.liberation.com/aubrac/page1.html.

Aubrac, Lucie. "Des éloges aux soupçons." *Libération*, July 10, 1997.

———. *Ils partiront dans l'ivresse*. Paris: Éditions du Seuil, 1984.

Aubrac, Raymond. "Ce que cette table-ronde m'a appris." *Libération*, July 10, 1997.

———. "Et si les historiens nous posaient des questions?" *Libération*, July 9, 1997.

Augustine, Saint. *Confessions*. Trans. R. S. Pine-Coffin. Baltimore: Penguin Books, 1961.

Azéma, Jean-Pierre, François Bédarida, and Robert Frank, eds. *Jean Moulin et la Résistance en 1943*. Forum in *Les Cahiers de l'IHTP* 27 (June 1994).

Bartov, Omer. *Murder in Our Midst: The Holocaust, Industrial Killing, and Representations*. New York: Oxford University Press, 1996.

———, ed. *The Holocaust: Origins, Implementation, Aftermath*. New York: Routledge, 2000.

Bédarida, François. "La dialectique passé/présent et la pratique historienne." In *L'Histoire et le Métier d'historien en France, 1945-1995*, ed. François Bédarida, 75-85. Paris: Éditions de la Maison des Sciences de l'Homme, 1995.

———. "Mémoire de la Résistance et devoir de vérité." *Libération*, July 12-13, 1997.

Berthomé, Jean-Marc. "Recherche psychanalytique sur la survivance des traumatismes concentrationnaire et génocidaire de la Seconde Guerre mondiale." 2 vols. Diss. Université de Paris-XI/Faculté de Médecine de Paris-Sud, 1997.

Birnbaum, Pierre. *La France imaginée: déclin des rêves unitaires?* Paris: Fayard, 1998. *The Idea of France.* Trans. M. B. DeBevoise. New York: Hill and Wang, 2001.

Bloch, Marc. *Apologie pour l'histoire ou métier d'historien.* Ed. Étienne Bloch. Pref. Jacques Le Goff. Paris: Armand Colin, 1998. *The Historian's Craft.* Trans. Peter Putnam. Intro. Joseph R. Strayer. New York: Vintage Books, 1964.

———. *Étrange défaite: témoignage écrit en 1940.* Paris: Éditions Gallimard, 1990. *Strange Defeat: A Statement of Evidence Written in 1940.* Trans. Gerard Hopkins. New York: Octagon Books, 1968.

———. "Que demander à l'histoire?" In *Histoire et historiens: textes réunis par Étienne Bloch,* 29–43. Paris: Armand Colin, 1995.

Boutier, Jean, and Dominique Julia, eds. *Passés recomposés: champs et chantiers de l'histoire.* Paris: Éditions Autrement, 1995.

Bracher, Nathan, ed. *A Time to Remember.* Special issue of *Contemporary French Civilization* 19, no. 2 (1995).

Cassirer, Ernst. *An Essay on Man: An Introduction to a Philosophy of Human Culture.* New Haven, Conn.: Yale University Press, 1972, 1992.

Chateaubriand, René de. *Mémoires d'outre-tombe* [1849–50]. 2 vols. Paris: Éditions Gallimard (Bibliothèque de la Pléiade), 1951.

Chaumont, Jean-Michel. *La concurrence des victimes: génocide, identité, reconnaissance.* Paris: La Découverte, 1997.

"Chirac Affirms France's Guilt in Fate of Jews." *New York Times,* July 17, 1995, A1, A3.

Conan, Éric. "Le procès Papon: il faut en finir!" *L'Express,* January 22–28, 1998, 10–15.

———. *Le procès Papon: un journal d'audience.* Paris: Éditions Gallimard, 1998.

Conan, Éric, and Daniel Lindenberg. "Pourquoi y a-t-il une affaire Jean Moulin?" In forum *Que reste-t-il de la Résistance? Esprit,* no. 198 (January 1994): 5–18.

———. "Que faire de Vichy." In forum *Que faire de Vichy? Esprit,* no. 181 (May 1992): 5–15.

Conan, Éric, and Henry Rousso. *Vichy, un passé qui ne passe pas* [1994]. Paris: Éditions Gallimard (Folio-Histoire), 1996. *Vichy: An Ever-Present Past.* Ed. and trans. Nathan Bracher. Foreword by Robert O. Paxton. Hanover, N.H.: University Press of New England, 1998.

Cordier, Daniel. " 'Je vous écris d'un pays lointain.' " *Libération,* July 11, 1997.

Courtois, Stéphane, Nicolas Werth, Jean-Louis Panné, Andrzej Paczkowski, Karel Bartosek, and Jean-Louis Margolin. *Le livre noir du communisme: crimes, terreur, répression.* Paris: Laffont, 1997. *The Black Book of Communism: Crimes, Terror, Repression.* Trans. Jonathan Murphy and Mark Kramer. Cambridge, Mass.: Harvard University Press, 1999.

Déak, István, Jan T. Gross, and Tony Judt, eds. *The Politics of Retribution in Europe.* Princeton, N.J.: Princeton University Press, 2000.

de Baecque, Antoine, and Christian Delage. *De l'histoire au cinéma.* Brussels/Paris: Éditions Complexe/IHTP-CNRS (Histoire du Temps Présent), 1998.

Delage, Christian, and Nicolas Rousselier, eds. *Cinéma, le temps de l'histoire.* Special issue of *Vingtième siècle: Revue d'histoire* 46 (April-June 1995).

Douzou, Laurent. "Les documents ne sont pas des électrons libres." *Libération,* July 12-13, 1997.

Farge, Arlette. *Des lieux pour l'Histoire.* Paris: Éditions du Seuil, 1997.

———. *Le goût de l'archive.* Paris: Éditions du Seuil, 1989.

Finkelstein, Norman G. *The Holocaust Industry: Reflection on the Exploitation of Jewish Suffering.* New York: Verso, 2000.

Finkielkraut, Alain. *La mémoire vaine: du crime contre l'humanité.* Paris: Éditions Gallimard, 1989. *Remembering in Vain: The Klaus Barbie Trial and Crimes Against Humanity.* Trans. Roxanne Lapidus and Sima Godfrey. New York: Columbia University Press, 1992.

———. "Papon: trop tard," *Le Monde,* October 14, 1997. "Papon: Too Late." In *Memory and Justice on Trial: The Papon Affair,* ed. Richard J. Golsan, trans. Lucy B. Golsan, 190–92. New York: Routledge, 2000.

Fishman, Sarah, et al. *France at War: Vichy and the Historians.* Trans. David Drake. New York: Berg, 2000.

Forum: The Vichy Syndrome. Special issue of *French Historical Studies* 19, no. 2 (fall 1995).

Frei, Norbert. *Vergangenheitspolitik: Die Anfänge der Bundesrepublik und die NS-Vergangenheit.* Munich: C. H. Beck, 1996.

Friedländer, Saul, ed. *Probing the Limits of Representation: Nazism and the "Final Solution."* Cambridge, Mass.: Harvard University Press, 1992.

Furet, François. *Le passé d'une illusion: essai sur l'idée communiste au XXe siècle.* Paris: Calmann-Lévy, 1995. *The Passing of an Illusion: The Idea of Communism in the Twentieth Century.* Trans. Deborah Furet. Chicago: University of Chicago Press, 1995.

Gallerano, Nicola. *L'uso publico della storia.* Milan: Franco Angeli, 1995.

Ginzburg, Carlo. *The Judge and the Historian: Marginal Notes on a Late Twentienth-Century Miscarriage of Justice.* Trans. Antony Shugaar. New York: Verso, 1999.

Golsan, Richard J. *Vichy's Afterlife: History and Counterhistory in Postwar France.* Lincoln: University of Nebraska Press, 2000.

———, ed. *Memory, the Holocaust, and French Justice: The Bousquet and Touvier Affairs.* Hanover, N.H.: University Press of New England, 1996.

———. *The Papon Affair: Memory and Justice on Trial.* New York: Routledge, 2000.

Gordon, Bertram M. "The 'Vichy Syndrome' Problem in History." *French Historical Studies* 19, no. 2 (fall 1995): 495–518.

Grosser, Alfred. *Le crime et la mémoire.* Paris: Flammarion, 1989.

Halbwachs, Maurice. *Les cadres sociaux de la mémoire* [1925]. Paris: Albin Michel, 1994. *On Collective Memory.* Trans. Lewis A. Coser. Chicago: University of Chicago Press, 1992.

———. *La mémoire collective* [1950]. Paris: Albin Michel, 1997. *The Collective Memory.* Trans. Francis J. Ditter Jr. and Vida Yazdi Ditter. New York: Harper Colophon Books, 1980.

Hegel, Georg W. F. *Lectures on the Philosophy of History* [1837]. Trans. H. B. Nisbet. Cambridge: Cambridge University Press, 1975, 1980.
———. *Philosophy of Right* [1821]. Trans. T. M. Knox. London: Oxford University Press, 1967.
Hellman, John. "Wounding Memories: Mitterand, Moulin, Touvier, and the Divine Half-Lie of Resistance." *French Historical Studies* 19, no. 2 (fall 1995): 461–86.
Hilberg, Raul. *The Politics of Memory: The Journey of a Holocaust Historian.* Chicago: Ivan R. Dee Press, 1996.
Institut d'Histoire du Temps Présent. *Écrire l'histoire du temps présent: en hommage à François Bédarida.* Paris: CNRS Éditions, 1993.
Jankélévitch, Vladimir. *L'imprescriptible: pardonner? Dans l'honneur et la dignité.* Paris: Éditions du Seuil, 1986.
Klarsfeld, Serge. *Le mémorial de la déportation des juifs de France.* Paris: Klarsfeld, 1978. *Memorial to the Jews Deported from France, 1942–1944: Documentation of the Deportation of the Victims of the Final Solution in France.* Trans. Violet Hellman. New York: Beate Klarsfeld Foundation, 1983.
———. *Le mémorial des enfants juifs déportés de France.* Paris: Les Fils et Filles des Déportés Juifs de France/Beate Klarsfeld Foundation, 1994. *French Children of the Holocaust: A Memorial.* Trans. Glorianne Depondt. New York: New York University Press, 1996.
Koselleck, Reinhart. *L'expérience de l'histoire.* Preface by Michael Werner. Trans. Alexandre Escudier et al. Paris: Hautes Études—Gallimard—Éditions du Seuil, 1997.
———. *Futures Past: On the Semantics of Historical Time* [1979]. Trans. Keith Tribe. Cambridge, Mass.: MIT Press, 1985.
Kritz, Neil J., ed. *Transitional Justice: How Emerging Democracies Reckon with Former Regimes.* Foreword by Nelson Mandela. Washington, D.C.: U. S. Institute of Peace Press, 1995.
Kritzman, Lawrence D., ed. *Auschwitz and After: Race, Culture, and the "Jewish Question" in France.* New York: Routledge, 1995.
Laborie, Pierre. "Historiens sous haute surveillance." *Esprit*, no. 198 (January 1994): 36–49.
Lagrou, Pieter. *The Legacy of Nazi Occupation: Patriotic Memory and National Recovery in Western Europe, 1945–1965.* Cambridge: Cambridge University Press, 1999.
Lavabre, Marie-Claire. "Du poids et du choix du passé: lecture critique du 'syndrome de Vichy.' " In *Histoire politique et sciences sociales*, ed. Denis Peschanski, Michael Pollak, and Henry Rousso, 265–78. Brussels: Éditions Complexe-IHTP, 1991.
———. *Le fil rouge: sociologie de la mémoire communiste.* Paris: Presses de la FNSP, 1994.
———. "Usages du passé, usages de la mémoire." *Revue française de science politique* 54, no. 3 (June 1994): 480–93.
Maier, Charles S. *The Unmasterable Past: History, Holocaust, and German National Identity.* Cambridge, Mass.: Harvard University Press, 1997.
Niethammer, Lutz. *Kollective Identität: Heimliche Quellen einer unheimlichen Konjunktur.* Hamburg: Rowohlt, 2000.

Nietzsche, Friedrich. *Unmodern Observations* [1873–74]. Trans. Gary Brown. New Haven, Conn: Yale University Press, 1990.

Noiriel, Gérard. "Les pairs dans l'impasse." *Le Monde de l'éducation*, November 11, 1997.

———. *Sur la "crise" de l'histoire*. Paris: Belin, 1996.

Nora, Pierre, ed. *Les lieux de mémoire*. Vol. 1: *La République*; Vol. 2: *La Nation*; Vol. 3: *Les France*. Paris: Éditions Gallimard, 1984, 1986, 1992. *Realms of Memory: Rethinking the French Past*. Trans. Arthur Goldhammer. Vol. 1: *Conflicts and Divisions*; Vol. 2: *Traditions*; Vol. 3: *Symbols*. New York: Columbia University Press, 1996–97.

———. "Le syndrome, son passé, son avenir." *French Historical Studies* 19, no. 2 (fall 1995): 487–93.

Novick, Peter. *The Holocaust in American Life*. New York: Houghton Mifflin, 1999.

Osiel, Mark. *Mass Atrocity, Collective Memory, and the Law*. New Brunswick, N.J.: Transaction, 1997.

Paxton, Robert O. *Vichy France: Old Guard and New Order, 1940–1944*. New York: Alfred Knopf, 1972.

Peschanski, Denis, Michael Pollak, and Henry Rousso, eds. *Histoire politique et sciences sociales*. Brussels: Éditions Complexe, 1991.

Pollak, Michael. *L'expérience concentrationnaire: essai sur le maintien de l'identité sociale*. Paris: Éditions Métailié, 1990.

Prost, Antoine. *Douze leçons sur l'histoire*. Paris: Éditions du Seuil (Points-Histoire) 1996.

Raulff, Ulrich. *De l'origine à l'actualité: Marc Bloch, l'histoire et le problème du temps présent*. Sigmaringen: Jan Thorbecke, 1997.

Rémond, René, et al. *Touvier et l'Église: rapport de la commission historique instituée par le Cardinal Decourtray*. Paris: Fayard, 1992.

Renan, Ernest. "What Is a Nation?" In *Becoming National: A Reader*, ed. and trans. Geoff Eley and Ronald Grigor Suny, 42–55. New York: Oxford University Press, 1996.

La responsabilité sociale de l'historien. Special issue of *Diogène* 168 (1994).

Ricœur, Paul. *La critique et la conviction: entretien avec François Azouvi et Marc de Launay*. Paris: Calmann-Lévy, 1995. *Critique and Conviction: Conversations with François Azouvi and Marc de Launay*. Trans. Kathleen Blamey. New York: Columbia University Press, 1998.

———. *La mémoire, l'histoire, l'oubli*. Paris: Éditions du Seuil, 2000.

———. *Temps et récit*. 3 vols. Paris: Éditions du Seuil, 1983–85. *Time and Narrative*. Trans. Kathleen McLaughlin and David Pellauer. Chicago: University of Chicago Press, 1984.

Rousso, Henry. "De l'usage du 'mythe-nécessaire.' " *Libération*, July 11, 1997.

———. "Le syndrome de l'historien." *French Historical Studies* 19, no. 2 (fall 1995): 519–26.

———. *Le syndrome de Vichy de 1944 à nos jours* [1987]. Paris: Éditions du Seuil (Points-Histoire), 1990. *The Vichy Syndrome: History and Memory in France Since 1944*. Trans. Arthur Goldhammer. Cambridge, Mass.: Harvard University Press, 1991, 1994.

———, ed. *Stalinisme et nazisme: histoire et mémoire comparées*. Brussels:

Éditions Complexe (Histoire du Temps Présent), 1999. *Nazism and Stalinism: History and Memory Compared.* Trans. Peter Rogers, Thomas Hildy, and Lucy B. Golsan. Lincoln: University of Nebraska Press, 2002.

Segev, Tom. *The Seventh Million: The Israelis and the Holocaust.* Trans. Haim Watzman. New York: Henry Holt, 1993, 2000.

Seignobos, Charles. *Histoire de la nation française: essai d'une histoire de l'évolution du peuple français.* Paris: Rieder-PUF, 1939.

Semprun, Jorge. *L'écriture ou la vie.* Paris: Éditions Gallimard, 1994. *Literature or Life.* Trans. Linda Coverdale. New York: Viking, 1997.

Shur, Emma. "Pédagogiser la Shoah?" *Le Débat* 96 (September-October 1997): 122–40.

Taguieff, Pierre-André. *L'effacement de l'avenir.* Paris: Galilée, 2000.

———. *Les fins de l'antiracisme.* Paris: Michalon, 1995.

Thibaud, Paul. "Un temps de mémoire?" *Le Débat* 96 (September-October 1997): 166–83.

Todorov, Tzvetan. *Les abus de la mémoire.* Paris: Arléa, 1995.

Veillon, Dominique. "Trouble-mémoire." *Libération,* July 11, 1997.

Vernant, Jean-Pierre. "Faut-il briser des idoles?" *Libération,* July 12–13, 1997.

Vidal-Naquet, Pierre. *Réflexions sur le génocide.* Vol. 3 of *Les Juifs, la mémoire et le présent.* Paris: La Découverte, 1995.

———. *Le trait empoisonné: réflexions sur l'affaire Jean Moulin.* Paris: La Découverte, 1993.

Voldman, Danièle, ed. *La bouche de la vérité? La recherche historique et les sources orales.* Special issue of *Les Cahiers de l'IHTP* 21 (November 1992).

Weill, Nicolas. "Le dilemme des historiens cités à comparaître." *Le Monde,* October 16, 1997.

Wieviorka, Annette. *Déportation et génocide: entre la mémoire et l'oubli.* Paris: Plon, 1992.

———. *L'ère du témoin.* Paris: Plon, 1999.

Wood, Nancy. *Vectors of Memory: Legacies of Trauma in Postwar Europe.* New York: Berg, 1999.

Yerushalmi, Yosef Hayim. *Zakhor: Jewish History and Jewish Memory.* Seattle: University of Washington Press, 1982, 1996.

Index